The Market's Morals

Responding to Jesse Norman

THE KAPUNDA PRESS

an imprint of Connor Court Publishing
in association with the PM Glynn Institute

Series editor:
Damien Freeman

PM Glynn Institute
Australian Catholic University

CHALICE OF LIBERTY
PROTECTING RELIGIOUS FREEDOM IN AUSTRALIA
Frank Brennan – M. A. Casey – Greg Craven

TODAY'S TYRANTS
RESPONDING TO DYSON HEYDON
Frank Brennan – Anne Henderson – Paul Kelly – M. A. Casey – Peter Kurti
M. J. Crennan – Hayden Ramsay – Shireen Morris – Michael Ondaatje
Sandra Lynch – Catherine Renshaw

FEDERATION'S MAN OF LETTERS
PATRICK MCMAHON GLYNN
Gerald O'Collins – Anne Henderson – John Fahey – Anne Twomey
Peter Boyce – Suzanne Rutland – Patrick Mullins

NONSENSE ON STILTS
RESCUING HUMAN RIGHTS IN AUSTRALIA
M. A. Casey – Damien Freeman – Catherine Renshaw – Nicholas Aroney
Emma Dawson – Terri Butler – Bryan S. Turner – Tim Wilson – Jennifer Cook

STORY OF OUR COUNTRY
LABOR'S VISION FOR AUSTRALIA
Adrian Pabst

Forthcoming:

THE NEW SOCIAL CONTRACT
RENEWING THE LIBERAL VISION FOR AUSTRALIA
Tim Wilson

The Market's Morals

Responding to Jesse Norman

Edited by Damien Freeman

CONNOR COURT PUBLISHING PTY LTD
PO Box 7257
Redland Bay QLD 4165
sales@connorcourt.com
www.connorcourt.com

Cover image: Detail from a wall painting, Drake House, Melbourne (St Patrick's) Campus, Australian Catholic University.

ISBN: 978-1-925826-76-0 (pbk.)

Cover design by Ian James

Printed in Australia

"Nobody ever saw a dog make a fair and deliberate exchange of one bone for another with another dog."

Adam Smith

CONTENTS

FOREWORD

ANTHONY FISHER

The word 'capitalism' is often used today to mean the idea that wealth and resources are the cause and source of human happiness and social morality. Whether accurate or as a summary of the theory of capitalism, this idea does great harm to our sense of social identity and, to use Jesse Norman's point, social order. This idea that we can do away with any sense of morality, obligation, and mutual interdependence is made all the more dangerous by its very vagueness, for an idea that can't be defined can't be critiqued. Jesse Norman, in his PM Glynn Lecture, notes that after the fall of the Berlin Wall, capitalism and the free market were thought to have won, and to have been proven supreme; yet, as we have seen in the decades since, profit cannot be turned to as the Saviour of humanity, and wealth will not do away with mistreatment of others.

In 1930, despite the Great Depression, the British economist John Maynard Keynes wrote optimistically about the *Economic Possibilities for our Grandchildren*.[1] He predicted that continued improvements in productivity would yield by today an average work-day of three hours, work-week of fifteen hours, and sufficient incomes to support greater leisure and security. Yet for all the productivity increases since Keynes's day—much greater than he imagined[2]—the benefits have been very unevenly shared, most work at least as many hours as people did decades ago, most families now need two bread-winners to make ends meet, many are now priced out of the housing market, and wages have been stagnant for some years.[3]

We might be tempted to say Keynes's story only shows how pointless it is to gaze three generations into the future. But was he wrong to want his grandchildren to share the benefits of rising productivity? If taxation or other economic reform comes, will it be on terms that assist such ordinary human aspirations to come to fruition, let alone the richer social and business ethic elaborated in the Christian tradition? Will all the stakeholders—owners, executives, workers, suppliers, customers, taxpayers—reasonably benefit? I say 'reasonably', because justice does not require all benefits be equally shared: even in heaven some people get better seats than others! But under our presently reigning business and governmental 'ethic', corporate gains may be enjoyed by shareholders and executives but not necessarily by workers or customers. Clearly more reflection is needed on the inseparable link between market and morality, for the very reason that a market serves a community, and there is no community without morality.

As its title suggests, the present book aims to raise these very issues. To have had someone with the intellect and experience of Jesse Norman to lead that conversation is yet another great achievement for the PM Glynn Institute. The other great minds of this volume critique and continue Norman's thought, extending the discussion further, probing deeper into the market's morality.

This book is an important contribution to that ongoing conversation around the role of the market in social order and morality, and I pray that it will be disseminated and read widely.

✠Anthony Fisher OP
Archbishop of Sydney
2019

INTRODUCTION

DAMIEN FREEMAN

It was near the intersection of Prince Albert Road and St Marys Road that the initial contact between the first and second PM Glynn Lecturers took place.

The first words spoken were, "I see they pick PM Glynn Lecturers on the basis of height."

I know this to be true for I was there when it was uttered and they both towered over me. The intellectual stature of J. D. Heydon QC and Jesse Norman MP is aptly embodied in their physical stature.

Although Norman is not the Wagnerian soprano from New York that some may have been expecting, he has an abiding interest in jazz and opera, which makes the cover image on this volume fitting. Two minstrels are depicted on a street corner, standing head-and-shoulders above their peers: a fitting tribute to the encounter at the corner of Prince Albert and St Marys, and a genteel retort to the image on the previous volume, in which the figure thought to represent Heydon eschewed the music-making in which he rejoices on the cover of this volume.

The Right Honourable Alexander Jesse Norman was born on 23 June 1962 in London to the businessman and philanthropist, Sir Torquil Norman CBE, and his wife, Lady Elizabeth Norman (née Montagu). He was educated at Eton College and won an

Open Exhibition to Merton College at the University of Oxford, where he graduated with a Bachelor of Arts in classics in 1985. He later received the degrees of Master of Philosophy (1999) and Doctor of Philosophy (2003) in philosophy from University College London.

His academic appointments included teaching fellow and lecturer (1998-2003) and honorary research fellow (2005-10) at University College London and lecturer at Birkbeck College London (2003). He was a visiting fellow at All Souls College, Oxford in 2016-17.

Outside academia, Dr Norman has held a variety of positions in finance and business, including as Director at BZW, part of Barclays Bank. In politics and public policy, he served as the inaugural executive director of Policy Exchange, one of the United Kingdom's leading think-tanks, from 2005 to 2006.

In 2010, he was elected as the Member of the House of Commons for Hereford and South Herefordshire, having been preselected as a parliamentary candidate for the Conservative party in 2006. He served as a member of the Treasury Committee from 2010 to 2015, before being elected by his fellow MPs as chairman of the House of Commons Select Committee on Culture, Media and Sport from 2015 to 2017.

Dr Norman was brought into the first May ministry in 2016 as Parliamentary Under-Secretary of State at the Department of Business, Energy and Industrial Strategy. In July 2017, when the second May ministry was formed, he was appointed Parliamentary Under-Secretary of State for Roads, Local Transport and Devolution, and subsequently Minister of State at the Department of Transport, before serving as Her Majesty's Paymaster-General and Financial Secretary to the Treasury from May 2019. He has continued to serve as Financial Secretary to the Treasury in the first and second Johnson ministries since July 2019, and was sworn of Her Majesty's Most Honourable Privy Council.

Dr Norman is the author of numerous books and pamphlets, including *The Achievement of Michael Oakeshott* (1992), *Breaking the Habits of a Lifetime: Poland's First Steps to the Market* (1992), *After Euclid: Visual Reasoning and the Epistemology of Diagrams* (2006), *Compassionate Conservatism* (2006), *Compassionate Economics* (2008), *Churchill's Legacy* (2009), and *The Big Society* (2010). His biography, *Edmund Burke: Philosopher, Politician, Prophet* was published to great acclaim in 2013. His latest book, *Adam Smith: What He Thought, and Why It Matters*, was published by Penguin Books in 2018.

Shortly before the publication of *Adam Smith*, Norman delivered the second PM Glynn Lecture on Religion, Law and Public Life. The lecture was established by Australian Catholic University's public policy think-tank, the PM Glynn Institute, to honour the contribution that its namesake, Patrick McMahon Glynn, made to Australia, both as one of the founding fathers of the Commonwealth, and as a prominent writer, lawyer, and parliamentarian. This annual lecture invites an eminent person to address an important question at the intersection of religion, law, and public life, with a view to enhancing the quality of discussion about important matters of public policy.

Dr Michael Casey, director of the PM Glynn Institute, wrote in the preface to a pamphlet containing the lecture, "Dr Norman is one of the distinguished polymaths of British parliamentary life. His lecture brings an acute philosophical sensibility and a deep sociological realism to bear on some critical questions of the moment. One of these questions is the nature and purpose of politics in a situation where we seem to be 'trapped in bleak and nihilistic narratives of grievance and anger' which 'ignore our history and devalue our society', and make it harder and harder for us to see what we have in common with those around us."

The second lecture was entitled "The moral basis of a commercial society", and it is reproduced at the beginning of this volume.

The lecture begins by drawing some comparisons between the experiences of the lecture's namesake in nineteenth-century Ireland and Edmund Burke in the eighteenth century. Burke is introduced as a theorist who can help us make sense of the breakdown and disintegration that seem to characterize modern society, especially in the Anglosphere, and there is a brief discussion of recent developments and broader political responses thereto which have contributed to the current climate. These problems might be analysed in purely economic terms, but it is suggested that to do so would be misguided. The problems that emerge are questions of social and political thought. Four approaches to addressing these problems are given short shrift: natural law, social contract theory that begins with Thomas Hobbes, Immanuel Kant's universal code of duties of free rational agents, and the utilitarianism of Jeremy Bentham and J. S. Mill. It is proposed that although these four traditions are not up to the challenge of addressing the problems that we currently face, there is another tradition that is capable of doing so, the tradition of "natural utility". The tradition of natural utility is said to have its genesis in the writings of Edmund Burke and Adam Smith. When Burke and Smith are read together, it is argued that they provide "a vision of society fit to sustain us for the long term". From Burke is taken an account of a social order understood in terms of "an enormous and ever-shifting web of institutions, customs, traditions, habits, and expectations built up by innumerable interactions over many centuries", and which are grounded in feelings of "affection, identity, and interest". From Smith is taken an account of commercial society, in which the famous thesis about markets, expounded in *The Wealth of Nations*, is situated in the context of a less well-known work, *The Theory of Moral Sentiments*, in which Smith develops an account of sympathy, which provides the basis for moral norms. The concept of natural utility emerges when these insights from Burke and Smith are combined and give rise to "the idea of commercial society", which "rests on mutual obligation and mutual esteem", and of which political leaders are custodians. Commercial society, it is argued, brings together markets and morals in a way that rejects market fundamentalism's approach to economics as a "value-free science". In doing so, it offers a distinctive model of political leadership and affirms the value of "social capital". In this way, it is proposed that current extreme instantiations of capitalism need to be reformed for the sake of preserving commercial society.

In the lecture, Norman makes several connections with the inaugural lecture, "Religious 'toleration' in modern Australia: the tyranny of relativism". That lecture was published with eleven responses in *Today's Tyrants: Responding to Dyson Heydon*. This volume follows suit by publishing the second lecture together with a collection of twelve responses. It is anticipated that the third lecture, "Overcoming political tribalism", delivered by Lord Williams of Oystermouth on 8 September 2019, will similarly be published together with a collection of responses in due course.

This collection begins with two responses considering Norman's treatment of the history of political thought. Marc Stears situates Norman's remarks in the context of D. H. Lawrence's novels, and suggests that we can see in Lawrence a yearning for a form of political life not unlike that sketched out by Norman. Adrian Pabst then examines the way Norman brings together Adam Smith and Edmund Burke to provide an account of natural utility.

The following essays move the volume into a discussion of Burke's significance in Australian history. Gregory Melleuish traces the significance of Burke for liberal and conservative parties in Australia, and Michael Easson makes a case for the Australian Labor Party as the true custodian of Burke's legacy in Australia.

Norman's thesis about commercial society comes under scrutiny in the next three essays. Amanda Walsh challenges Norman's claim that the left has failed to address the big issues in political economy, and argues that, at least in the Australian context, Labor has provided a more credible alternative than Norman's commercial society. Leanne Smith offers a more wide-ranging critique, arguing that Norman's idea of natural utility cannot meet the challenge that he identifies, although she maintains that social democracy can deliver where natural utility does not. Cris Abbu completes the critical commentary with a narrower commentary, in which she points out that, even if commercial society is beneficial in markets where there is ceaseless exchange, it cannot deal adequately with thin markets, in which individuals do not find themselves presented with a marketplace offering a multitude of options from which they can freely choose; a situation exemplified in Australia by the National Disability Insurance Scheme.

The next four essays take Norman's lecture as a departure point for a range of issues raised by contemporary society, including the significance of partnerships, the millennials' attachment to socialism, the nature of leadership, and the values of a university operating in a marketplace. David Corbett finds in Norman's use of Adam Smith the basis for advocating partnership as the cornerstone of a moral and economic order that is superior to the alternatives offered by communism and capitalism. Parnell McGuinness draws inspiration from Norman's vision of commercial society, which she believes might hold the key for rescuing political leadership from the managerialism that currently dominates the conduct of the political class. Tom Switzer sees in Norman's take on Burke and Smith some hope for a conservative response to the challenge of millennials, who seem eager to embrace socialism in the absence of any compelling defence of liberal institutions. Tania Aspland uses Norman's account of commercial society as a vehicle for thinking about some of the challenges presented by the values that come into conflict when one venerable institution, the university, finds itself having to survive within another venerable institution, the marketplace.

The volume concludes with an essay by Michael Casey, in which he argues that Norman offers us a sobering antidote to the imminent threat of an era plagued by new forms of extreme radical ideology. Norman's commercial society, he suggests, is a model for social life in which self-restraint enables contempt to give way to respect for people and their attachments, for the social order, and the achievements of the past. As such, it offers a source of hope for our life in common.

Like Burke, Norman has combined his time in the Palace of Westminster with more philosophical pursuits. Like Norman, Glynn revered Burke, and this reverence was well known in Melbourne, where the *Argus* declared in 1905, "Mr Glynn is a student of his great countryman, Edmund Burke, and in breadth and loftiness of ideas, as in the beauty and purity of language, he is not unworthy of his master." It took another century for Sydney to cotton on, when Norman delivered his lecture on Burke and Smith in the crypt of St Mary's Cathedral on 9 April 2018, after which the Glynn Lecturer received the hospitality of His Grace the Archbishop of Sydney at the Cathedral House. And so it came to pass that, from the depths of the crypt of the mother church of Australia, the light of Glynn and Burke poured forth from the mouth of Norman.

The Second PM Glynn Lecture on

Religion, Law and Public Life

THE MORAL BASIS OF A COMMERCIAL SOCIETY

JESSE NORMAN

It is a great honour to be invited to give the second PM Glynn Lecture on Religion, Law and Public Life. This is my first visit to Australia, but as a former academic, I have also long been dazzled by this country—not by its natural beauty, but by the quality of its philosophers. Now to many Brits the mention of this subject will raise a smile: they will think of the Monty Python sketch of Australian philosophers all named Bruce, who want to name their English visitor Bruce "in order to avoid confusion". But the real laugh is on Monty Python, because when I worked in the subject at University College London twenty years ago we revered Australian philosophers such as John Mackie, David Armstrong, John Finnis, and Brian O'Shaughnessy, to say nothing of adopted Australians such as Jack Smart and David Lewis, and their many influential students and successors.

Those voices were very powerful in that small but wide-ranging world, but they were not merely powerful. These were tough-minded thinkers, and from metaphysics to logic to ethics they threw themselves at some of the hardest and most technically complex issues in the field. And above all, they were highly original. In the sixteenth and seventeenth centuries, the Latin phrase *In terra australis*—in the land of the south—was a standard form of words used to denote mythical and unknown places, of vast immensity and possibility, places in which, as they say, the hand of man had never set foot.

That idea—that things might be possible in Australia that would not be possible anywhere else in the world—persisted in philosophy. Little wonder that at one point the academic joke went that the phrase 'in Australia' was logically equivalent to the word 'not'. So one might say 'In Australia there are mammals that lay eggs', meaning of course that there are no such mammals in reality; or 'In Australia there are black swans', meaning that no real swans are black; or, in that complacent English way, 'In Australia people who stand upright have their heads pointing downwards', meaning perhaps that life down under inevitably stretches the limits of logic itself. I cannot comment on that; but I will say that we seem to be getting quite expert in logic-stretching ourselves back in Blighty at the moment.

I make no apologies, therefore, for taking an Australian audience, let alone one as distinguished as this, into—you must excuse me—some thorny thickets of theoretical thought.

But I am keenly aware too that it is an honour—and something of a challenge—to be asked to follow last year's immensely distinguished inaugural lecture by Justice Heydon. As he noted, Paddy Glynn's life showed what a career could lie open to a Catholic of real talent, despite serious headwinds of prejudice and circumstance, in nineteenth-century Ireland and then in the Australian colonies. We celebrate that talent, that life, and that career this evening; as those of the last of the Australian founders to sit in the Commonwealth Parliament, a leading voice among those who drafted the Bill of 1900, and of the reported author of the words "humbly relying on the blessing of Almighty God" in the Preamble to the Australian Constitution.

But there are real similarities with the life of another Irishman a century earlier, a man who—at a time when conventional opinion held that an Irishman in England was either after your fortune or your daughter—overcame discrimination and prejudice through raw talent, to make it to the very centre of British politics.

I refer of course to my great political hero, Edmund Burke. Burke was often accused by his political enemies of being a crypto-Catholic, and in cartoons he was often caricatured as a thin figure wearing the black coat and corned hat or *biretta* of the Jesuits, sometimes with a potato or a rosary to ram the point home. In fact, Burke was not himself a Catholic. But he came from a Catholic family on his mother's side, and this combined with his father's Protestantism and his own early education by the Quakers to give him a deep understanding of religious doctrine and practice. Religion apart, however, it is striking to note the many parallels between Burke and Glynn. Both were Irish, of course, both educated at Trinity College Dublin and both sent to the Middle Temple to study law. Both were renowned for their capacity for hard work; both expressed political views that were often controversial; both had a hatred of injustice; both were great constitutionalists, extraordinarily well read, and brilliant speakers. And whether in England or Australia, neither lost his Irish accent. It was said of Glynn that the more eloquent his speech, the thicker did his brogue become. It was said of Burke that he spoke with an accent "as strong as if he had never quitted the banks of the Shannon"—which itself perfectly illustrates English ignorance, since Burke was born on the banks of the Liffey, in Dublin.

My subject this evening is what I have called, adapting a phrase of the great Edward Banfield, the moral basis of a commercial society. I hope you will agree that this is a subject worthy of exploration, and perhaps especially so tonight since the Glynn Lecture is specifically dedicated to religion, law, and the public life, all areas which my title encompasses. You will understand, of course, that I am speaking here as someone who tries to write and think about philosophy and history and politics, not as a Member of Parliament, let alone as a Government minister.

And I hope you will agree that this subject is topical, for we seem to have become gripped in recent years by a kind of moral panic about the nature of modern society, especially in what is sometimes referred to as the Anglosphere. In Britain, this can be seen in the huge concern at current levels of drug abuse, loneliness, obesity, suicide, divorce, single motherhood, and teenage pregnancy. It can be seen in concern about falling social mobility and the future (or lack of it) for young people; in anger at economic and educational division, and what are seen as entrenched and self-selecting elites; in the remarkable distrust of traditional sources of authority; and in the suspicion that those in power are distant, unaccountable, and incapable of leadership. And it can be seen in culture wars over sexuality and gender, in fears of a loss of local or national identity, and in the escalating belief that hard-heartedness is now a norm, and that basic values of respect, hard work, and public service are being lost in celebrity worship, consumerism, and the money culture.

Much of the blame for these developments has been laid at the feet of free trade and the capitalist system. On this view, such things simply serve to worsen economic inequality and encourage corruption and greed. And all the more so, the argument goes, in an increasingly globalised world: a world in which capital is financialised, marketised, and liquid; companies are multinational and effectively able to choose where they pay tax; and labour is offshored to low-cost jurisdictions with few rights or union protections, while the rich are mobile and can relocate as and where they see fit. This in turn supports an emergent global value system which exalts material success; a brand-driven bucket-shop mentality that tacitly despises national cultures and local values and institutions.

In Britain—I cannot speak for Australia, of course—the broader political response to these concerns has moved from denial to division. After the fall of the Berlin Wall in 1989, there was remarkable complacency across the political spectrum about the status of capitalism, especially in the United Kingdom and the United States. History had supposedly ended, and free markets had won. The political centre-right largely fell back into a complacent snooze of self-satisfaction, while the centre-left refused to interfere with its quest for political power, and made its peace with the new dispensation—so much so that in the title of one influential book of the period, Tony Blair and Gordon Brown were "Thatcher's Children". The centre-right did not deem it necessary to make the case for the market economy in any serious way, let alone to develop the kind of systematic account of its strengths and weaknesses that might enable it to address public concerns about crony capitalism; while the centre-left neglected to offer any serious critique of its own, let alone to prepare for the negative effects of globalisation.

The public mood decisively changed with the financial crisis of 2007-08; with stagnating incomes, weak productivity, Occupy Wall Street, 'We are the 99%', and the work of the French economist Thomas Piketty in his best-selling book, *Capital in the 21st Century*. But the mainstream political response remained perilously weak. The right continued to repeat the language of 'free markets' from its 1980s heyday, without noticing that that phrase had all but lost its content, while the left simply seemed confused. Politics itself started to fracture horizontally, between urban and rural, young and old, more and less heavily educated, as different politicians sought to use nationalist and patriotic appeals to create and mobilize new coalitions of voters over the issue of European Union membership. Nudged by technology, tribes started to form that talked more and more not to others, but to themselves. The centre ground of British politics began to empty. Yet these phenomena were not exclusive to Britain: similar forces have been seen in many countries and many societies around the world. Is it any wonder, then, that the way has been open to more radical arguments and movements? Is it any wonder that extreme schemes of nationalisation, expropriation, and state control have begun to gain public currency?

Many of these issues have revolved around economics. But it would, I suggest, be a serious error to think about them merely in economic terms. At root, they concern basic questions of identity and legitimacy. They force us to ask once again: What is the nature of modern society? What sustains it? Why should we give it our continued loyalty as citizens, as individuals, as human beings? Why should we help others outside our immediate families and friends? Why should we make any sacrifice for others, come to that, if we have nothing in common with them? And who is this *we*, anyway?

As you will be aware, within the Western tradition, there have been many attempts to address these questions over the past four hundred years. But what counts as an answer has changed. Today, in heavily secularised societies dominated by the cultural pre-eminence of the sciences, we must answer these questions realistically, reflecting how people actually think and behave; and in a sober recognition that, for many people, traditional answers based on religious belief will not suffice. One may welcome that fact, or deplore it, as Justice Heydon so eloquently did in his lecture last year. But if an answer is to be generally persuasive, it has to do what many regard as impossible: take a description of the world, and somehow derive normative conclusions from it. It must extract the rich, warm blood of human value from the cold stone of bare fact.

At the risk of horrendous over-simplification, historically, there have been at least four approaches to these questions. The first is couched in terms of natural law: that human society is grounded via human nature in a grant from God or nature itself. The second derives from Thomas Hobbes, and argues that human society is based on a contract whereby individuals in a state of nature give up some of their personal autonomy to a sovereign power which guarantees their internal and external security in return. The third is the Kantian idea that human society is underwritten by a moral code of universal duties to which humans are committed just in virtue of being rational beings. And the final approach is the classical utilitarian idea that human society is legitimate only in so far as it conduces to individual wellbeing, and in particular the greatest good of the greatest number.

But I am now going to cut through these four hundred years of history and many thousands of volumes of political thought, by suggesting that while all the four approaches I have outlined have their attractions, none is adequate to the task before us. The natural law view rests on assumptions about a transcendent God or nature which many people, especially young people today, do not share. The social contract theory is a beguiling one, but it argues in a circle. For, as David Hume pointed out, how could human society derive from the promise contained in a social contract if people did not *already* accept a norm that promises should be honoured? And if they already accepted the validity of promises, why is it necessary to posit a social contract at all? It is a devastating attack. The Kantian approach fares no better, because it is unrealistic in its ethical demands and in its indifference to community. And nor does utilitarianism, a doctrine in which the one supreme good is the satisfaction of human wants, regardless of place or context.

But if these four sets of ideas are unavailing—if natural law, social contract, Kantian duty, and utilitarianism cannot afford us the answers we need—then where can we go? What is to be done?

My answer is this: that there is a fifth tradition, to be found in the writings of Edmund Burke and Adam Smith. We might call it the tradition of natural utility. It has escaped academic notice hitherto for reasons that need not detain us. But it gives us what we want, and vastly more: indeed, I believe it contains a vision of society fit to sustain us for the long term.

Let us start with Burke, and start where Burke starts. Not with some supposed state of nature but with the here and now, with what is given: with the fact of human society itself. Human beings grow up within human society, and their identities, behaviour, and institutions are formed by social interaction. Societies differ in many and various ways—rich or poor, open or closed, centralised or dispersed, warlike or peaceable. But each has a social order, which links people together in an enormous and ever-shifting web of institutions, customs, traditions, habits, and expectations built up by innumerable interactions over many years. Thus in eighteenth-century England, the social order would include the great estates of the realm: the monarchy, the aristocracy, and the commons; the 'establishments', such as the Church of England and the universities; the City of London, the guilds, and trading companies; the institutions of local government; the navy and army; the legal system and judiciary, and so on. But by extension it would also include the institutions surrounding marriage, birth, and death; church attendance and prayer; the tavern and the theatre; the arts and culture; booksellers and the press; gambling, drinking, and 'the mob'; and patterns of education, self-enrichment, and social mobility.

These institutions are ultimately grounded in feeling and emotion, which guide and direct man's reason. They are bound together by affection, identity, and interest. They matter for three reasons. First, they constrain each other, competing and co-operating as required to survive, diffusing power across communities, and providing a social challenge to state power. Secondly, they give shape and meaning to people's lives, at work or play, setting rhythms to the day or year, creating overlapping identities and personal loyalties. As Burke famously says in the *Reflections on the Revolution in France*: "to be attached to the subdivision, to love the little platoon we belong to in society, is . . . the first link in the series by which we proceed towards a love to our country, and to mankind." Finally, institutions trap and store knowledge. Composed of a myriad of private interactions, traditions, and practices as it is, the social order overall becomes a repository of shared knowledge and inherited wisdom.

The social order is not, then, the result of any overall design. It is not the outcome of any specific plan or project. It evolves slowly over time. Different social orders may evolve in different ways, and some may be more effective and successful than others. Each is *sui generis*, a largely accidental and historically contingent human achievement. It therefore makes an enormous difference how exactly each has evolved, and how it functions. Any practical or theoretical reflection on such a human artefact—and this applies to any institution, large or small, to peoples and nations as much as to words or ideas—must therefore begin with history and experience.

For Burke the social order is, in the language of the *Philosophical Enquiry into the Origin of our Ideas of the Sublime and Beautiful*, sublime: it far outstrips human understanding, triggering the instinct for self-preservation, and so feelings of awe and humility, in those who seek to grasp it. It is an inheritance, which imposes on each generation the obligation to preserve and if possible enhance it, before passing it on to the next generation. And there is no opt-out. In the words of the *Reflections*:

> Society is indeed a contract . . . but the state ought not . . . to be dissolved by the fancy of the parties. It is to be looked on with other reverence. . . . It is a partnership in all science, in all art, a partnership in every virtue and in all perfection. As the ends of such a partnership cannot be obtained in many generations, it becomes a partnership not only between those who are living, but between those who are living, those who are dead, and those who

are to be born.

So far, so good, ladies and gentlemen. But there is a problem. Burke's is an astonishingly powerful vision, a miracle of insight and rhetoric, but it is an outline. We need to see the inner workings better, and we need to understand how any of this can be relevant to our present lives.

For this purpose, we need to call on Adam Smith. But this is not just the Smith of that masterpiece of political economy, *The Wealth of Nations*; it is also the Smith of his little-known first book, *The Theory of Moral Sentiments*. Burke was a great admirer of that work, and from that admiration arose a long and close friendship between the two men. There are points of difference between the two, of course, but Smith reportedly believed that Burke was "the only man, who, without communication, thought on economic subjects exactly as he did", and this hints at a deeper and recognised affinity. Together, they are an extraordinary pair. Burke is the first great theorist of modern political parties and representative government. Smith is the first thinker to put markets at the centre of political economy, and so of economics, and to place norms at the centre of what we now think of as sociology. As Burke is the hinge of our political modernity, so is Smith the hinge of our economic, and in many ways our social, modernity. Theirs are momentous achievements.

Smith is sometimes accounted the father of capitalism, but I believe this is a serious mistake. For Smith, the central fact of his time in Britain was not the existence of what we would call capitalism, which did not emerge until the emergence of corporations as autonomous pools of capital in the mid-nineteenth century. Rather, it was the fact that feudalism had been superseded by what Smith called 'commercial society', a process which had unleashed huge prosperity, spreading wealth and replacing personal subordination with economic relationships of interdependence. In such a society, he says, "Every man . . . lives by exchanging, or becomes, in some measure, a merchant," as people seek to "better their condition" and autonomously create mutual obligations with each other.

But these processes of exchange are not merely economic; they are also moral. Like Burke, Smith sees man as a social animal, a being whose nature is to be in society. Indeed, there is little or no sense at all to be attached to the idea of man as an atom, wholly cut off from human society: the human self is a social self. Precisely for this reason, however, he argues that moral values and standards come not from the inside out, but from the outside in. They do not derive from divine revelation or some innate inner moral sense, but are created by human interaction itself. Humans naturally identify with each other imaginatively; they see each other's actions, and by means of what Smith calls 'sympathy' they come to see themselves as judgeable by others, and so come to judge their own conduct. Moreover, they seek "not only to be loved, but to be lovely; or to be that thing which is the natural and proper object of love"—and not only to be admired but to be worthy of admiration by others. This mutual interaction and empathy, corrected by what Smith calls the 'impartial spectator', becomes the basis for moral norms. Once a norm is established—be it a moral norm of personal integrity and truth-telling, or a social norm of good manners or fair dealing, it takes on a public life of its own and becomes authoritative to others. In effect, fact leads to value via norms.

We are now in a position to put Burke and Smith together. The moral basis of commercial society lies in the ceaseless exchange of mutual obligations and personal regard. In markets, this creates wealth and the benefits of spontaneous economic order; more widely, it creates ethical and social norms of behaviour. Both in turn generate habits, practices, and institutions. Cities, trade, manufactures, and commercial contracts come to the fore. Legal institutions emerge to adjudicate on and protect claims to property rights, and then rights more generally. The nature of criminal justice changes from direct individual or familial redress and compensation to a focus on the impact of crime on society as such, with a growing state monopoly of adjudication and enforcement. People become more civilised and pacific, and the collective demand for society to be orderly becomes of central importance. As the needs of society grow stronger, so too do society's demands on the state. This is a dynamic and evolutionary analysis that can be run at every level of human society, from the family to the community to the nation, and beyond.

It is important to be clear, though, that this picture does not offer a panacea. There will be societies in which the boot-strapping process by which freedom creates freedom cannot take place, because not enough of its people have boots on their feet at all. There will be societies in which that process runs slowly; and there will be institutions such as cartels and gangs which become dominated by norms that are expedient but anti-social. Sometimes this can happen to whole countries, as the history of fascism and communism reminds us: when they are controlled and directed to some purpose such as political conformity, national destiny, racial purity, or, today, extreme religious orthodoxy. It is part of the evil of these enforced communities that they are able to exploit what is perhaps the deepest human need—the need for meaning—to usurp and displace the freedoms of commercial society, freedoms which can all too easily be taken for granted. Indeed, one hesitates to call them societies in the true sense at all, because the equal status and freedoms implicit in the idea of a society have been subsumed by the hierarchies and structures of an overwhelming collective goal.

By contrast, the idea of commercial society rests on mutual obligation and mutual esteem. Its virtues are those of hard work, enterprise, creativity, and thrift, though Smith is also realistic about its vices. But such a society's sense of virtue is not simply that of the marketplace. On the contrary—and here we must turn back to Burke—it preserves a sense of the divine, in the need to respect something apart from and above oneself, something that gives a higher meaning and a moral perspective to human lives. It does this through the proper feeling of awe that any thinking person has and should have for the complexity and value of society itself as an inheritance; as Glynn puts it, "humbly relying on the blessing of Almighty God". It is in part the function of free institutions, as stores of memory and of politics, as channels for the articulation and reconciliation of conflicting views and interests, to be that national treasury of shared history and self-understanding. It is in part the function of political leaders to act as its custodians, to make that understanding a living force across the life and span of a nation. And it is in part the function of government to lift human capabilities and their free expression, and cherish moderation, tolerance, and mutual respect; its goal not merely private freedoms but a free and educated public realm, filled with the conversation of civil, honest, and independent minds.

So, then: why does all this matter? First, it reminds us that ultimately markets and morals cannot be separated from each other, for both rely on the human capacity for empathy and exchange. As Smith says, "Nobody ever saw a dog make a fair and deliberate exchange of one bone for another with another dog." Like all human institutions, markets rely on human acquiescence or consent. And so the idea that economics is, or could ever be, a value-free science is a hopeless one. As an ideology, market fundamentalism is dead.

Secondly, it offers an important but undervalued model of political leadership. On this view, the purpose of politics is not to satisfy the felt needs of any individual or generation; it is to preserve and enhance the social order in the public interest. It is therefore rooted in a sense of history. Leadership begins in respect for the social order, and so in modesty. It pushes leaders towards a close study of their people, all the people, and their institutions. It locates the 'we' of politics at the level of the nation as a whole. And it insists on the common good, and the importance of public service and public duty. In Burke's memorable words:

> We are afraid to put men to live and trade each on his own private stock of reason; because we suspect that this stock in each man is small, and that the individuals would do better to avail themselves of the general bank and capital of nations and of ages.

But thirdly, it is that idea of capital, of social capital, that is perhaps the most important. At least in the United Kingdom and America we seem to be becoming increasingly trapped in bleak and nihilistic narratives of grievance and anger, narratives that ignore our history and devalue our society. In his own time, Burke returned again and again to the idea of capital to explain what had gone wrong. As he said of the English Jacobins at the time of the French Revolution:

> You had all these advantages in your ancient states; but you chose to act as if you had never been moulded into civil society, and had everything to begin anew. You began ill, because you began by despising everything that belonged to you. You set up your trade without a capital.

Exactly the same thing could be said today.

Ladies and gentlemen, it is time for us to renew that capital. It is time to recover that shared understanding of what makes our countries today, each in its own ways, so remarkable: to ask what draws people towards our countries, and how we can continue in Smithian style to be worthy of the admiration of others in future. It is time to re-examine, and perhaps redefine, that 'we'—that partnership between those who are living, those who are dead, and those who are to be born—so that it spreads as widely and inclusively as possible today. And it is time to recognise that what matters about the modern era is not so much capitalism as commercial society itself. It is commercial society that, in its democratic form, has proven to have a unique capacity to command the allegiance of citizens, and to sustain its legitimacy over centuries by increasing their prosperity and freedom. This is an evolved collective achievement of extraordinary value, which it is the duty of us all to protect and enhance. Capitalism has its own pathologies—crony capitalism in all its many forms—and if the preservation of commercial society requires the reform of capitalism, then reform it we must. For the alternatives, of war over trade, of religious autocracy, authoritarian communism, and nationalism over democracy, or simply of an empty economic materialism, are not to be contemplated. And to those who argue that today's state-first models of capitalism are not merely ideologically but practically superior to commercial society, I say this: let us see what sources of legitimacy, what institutions, what mutual obligations bind such societies together when economic growth starts to slow, as it inevitably must. That, I think, will be a moment of reckoning.

Ladies and Gentlemen, as I have said, I cannot speak about Australia. I cannot speak to the vicissitudes and glories of national development and nation-building here over two centuries, and so I must leave it to you to tell me whether, and how far, what I have said may apply to this wonderful country. But let me suggest that when Paddy Glynn arrived in Australia in 1880, when he joined the Adelaide law firm of Hardy & Davis in 1882 and opened a branch office in Kapunda, when he became the editor of the *Kapunda Herald* in the following year and, above all, as Assemblyman, as delegate to the federal convention, and as Representative, he was acting in precisely the ways anticipated by Burke and Smith. Transacting commercial and political business, building a family, embedding himself in local institutions, campaigning and lobbying and always making the argument. It is a record anyone could be proud of, and one which it is an honour for me to celebrate with you tonight.

RESPONDING TO JESSE NORMAN

1

A POLITICS OF

EVERYDAY REALITY

MARC STEARS

Jesse Norman is a true conservative and that currently makes him a very rare breed indeed. At a time when politicians and intellectuals of the right rush towards projects of ever greater ambition and disruption, Norman reminds of the true benefits of conservative thinking. He places emphasis on the values that ought to be at the core of a conservative disposition: moderation, toleration, mutual concern, and a belief that good social outcomes—truly common goods—are most likely to emerge not when people are dictated to by powerful others, like distant government agencies, but when virtuous people are permitted to negotiate their own individual and collective solutions to the problems that life throws in their way. In his lecture on "The moral basis of a commercial society", Norman outlines all of this not only in beautiful prose, but with all of the breathtaking philosophical depth and historical range to which his avid readers have become accustomed.

What makes Norman's lecture so important today, however, is not that it is an argument made so well, but that it is an argument made at all. For modern-day political conservatives have largely lost faith in conservatism. Not for them, the call to combine "empathy with enterprise" that characterises Norman's vision. Instead, they are more likely to advance at least one of two alternative positions. Either, that is, they are *market fundamentalists* who believe everything will really be all right—the economy, the climate, our society—if we just leave the market to sort it out, or they are *cultural nationalists*—those wrapped up in some purist ideal of the nation state, or of Western civilisation, who are willing to denounce people of alternative backgrounds, or those who support alternative viewpoints, as not truly members of the same nation state. Norman's account owes nothing to either of these two approaches. Both of them would have appalled both Smith and Burke. But nor does he honestly acknowledge their power within his own political party or the larger political movement of which it is a part. "The moral basis of a commercial society", in other words, is a lecture that speaks powerfully of a conservatism that is now in the political wilderness, but which steadfastly refuses to acknowledge its current location. The key questions which I believe it leaves us with, therefore, are: why has the conservative tradition of which Norman speaks so eloquently so few current adherents in the actual politics of most developed democracies? And, what should those who remain attracted to it actually *do* in the polarised and very un-conservative times in which we live?

As a British citizen now living and working in Australia, I am always tempted to seek answers to these kind of questions in the great novel of British-Australian political disillusionment: D. H. Lawrence's *Kangaroo*. Lawrence had grown tired of the United Kingdom in World War I. He had no time for the bombast and the narrow-mindedness of a country at war. He left for Italy, but arrived there just in time to witness the rise of Mussolini and the Fascists and that held no appeal for him either. He came to Australia, imagining that perhaps here in a new country he would find a new politics. Blind as most of the English were to the horrors that had befallen the Aboriginal peoples, Lawrence thought that

Australia might be the most democratic nation of all. "In Australia", he wrote, "nobody is supposed to rule, and nobody does rule... The only source of authority . . . [is] the will of the people." "The instinct of the place [is] absolutely and flatly democratic, a *terre* democratic," he continued. "No need to get the wind up at all over it; it [is] a granted condition of Australia, that Demos [is] his own master."

Despite his initial optimism, however, Lawrence detected the same two precise flaws in Australian political life that he had diagnosed elsewhere, and intriguingly they are the same two flaws that I believe haunt conservatives today. The first flaw was what I shall call *denial*. The world was a mess at the end of World War I, Lawrence thought. Blighted by decade upon decade of raw industrialization, countries around the world were witnessing deeper and deeper class conflict. Economic inequality was becoming increasingly intense and environmental degradation was more and more notable. Capitalism had built a "world of iron and coal, the cruelty of iron and the smoke of coal," Lawrence insisted, and "endless, endless greed . . . drove it all." And the war had revealed the truth of it in its barest bones: "the cataclysm has happened, we are now among the ruins." And yet, despite this so many people in elite politics, Lawrence argued, had nothing serious to say about any of this. They continued as if everything was entirely fine; that an unreformed capitalism would correct the ship in time, that wealth would trickle down, that the environment would protect itself.

For Lawrence, the second flaw came from the opposite extreme. I call this the flaw of *purism*. These were the people who believed that if only the state could commit itself to some absolute goal and pursue it resolutely and without compromise all would be well. There was no shortage of purism in Lawrence's time. There were communists, socialists, fascists, nationalists; those who wanted to place religion at the heart of political life and those who wanted to expel faith altogether from the public square. What all of them had in common was moral certainty. They believed that they had *the* answer; the single pure solution to the world's ills. If only the world was not too stupid not to listen.

Lawrence had no time for any of that either. For him, the purists were no better that those who lived in denial. They hid from reality, just as those in denial did, but this time they hid in their fantasies, in their ideal abstractions. They told themselves utterly imagined stories about why it would all be all right in the end. "This is all the trouble", Lawrence explained exasperatedly, "that the invented *ideal* world of man is superimposed upon living men and women". "Socialism, conservatism, bolshevism, liberalism, republicanism, communism: all alike", he insisted. "They never live on the spot where they *are*. . . . They inhabit abstract space, the desert void of politics." They are captivated by things which do not really matter because they are derived from worlds that cannot be.

Kangaroo is the story of Lawrence's desperate effort to find a politics that escapes both of these two flaws. Lawrence longs for a politics which exhibits neither the *denial* of the market fundamentalists—the men in suits who believe everything will right itself—nor the empty abstract *purism* of those tempted by the grand illusions of the big ideologies—be they cultural reactionaries or socialist revolutionaries. Lawrence, in other words, is searching for a politics not unlike that which Jesse Norman sketches in his essay. He wants rid of the belief that markets do not need morals and he wants rid too of the belief that if only we could purify the nation somehow, by reclaiming an imagined sovereignty, perhaps, or ridding a nation of its immigrants, then some political perfection can be attained.

As anyone who has read it will remember, *Kangaroo* ends in despair. The married couple, of whom Lawrence writes in the novel, depart these shores having flirted with both the far right and the far left but having found no satisfaction in either. "Sydney, and the warm harbor. They crossed over once more in the blue afternoon," Lawrence writes. "Sydney lying on its many-lobed blue harbor, in the Australian spring" might have looked beautiful but his conclusion was that everything in his journey had failed. No salvation had been discovered. "Nothing could ever matter." It is not a book to read if you need cheering up. Lawrence's life after *Kangaroo* was spent arguing that those interested in the values that lie at the heart of any decent social creed—generosity of spirit, mutual concern, human energy, enterprise—should turn away from political life altogether and seek them in the form of immediate social interaction.

Despite the eventual pessimism, however, I hope it is clear why a turn to Lawrence can help make sense of our own times. Almost one hundred years on, I believe the challenges we face are astonishingly similar. Just as Lawrence noted, we have no shortage of politicians in denial. They are the market fundamentalists with nothing to say about inequality, social alienation, climate. And we have no shortage of purists either, on the right or the left. Head onto a university campus at a lunchtime, and you will be surrounded by those who preach the 'alternative' of socialist economic planning and you will also see those who profess blind faith in an alternative of closed borders and a return to 'Western Civilisation'. Just as in the early twentieth century, too, these purists are absolutists. Passionately uninterested in those who live around them but who see things in a different way. And unsuited to the task of enhancing our democracy as a result. So, just as in Lawrence's time, today we are confronted with two dominant ways of doing politics. One that denies the scale of the challenges that we face. Another that indulges in empty abstractions, so-called bold solutions which are in reality anything but.

The challenge is to see if there's anything *else* available—here in Australia—that might provide a different course, one far closer to the vision that Norman sketches in his essay. Such an alternative begins, I believe, in a place that Jesse Norman knows well: reality. Or rather, the everyday reality of everyday people. This is where the wisdom needed to make the changes we need actually resides. For too long, the experts of officialdom and business have said that the challenges we face can only be understood by those who enjoy positions of authority within an established order. But experience has revealed the folly in this view. In fact, it is only by listening to the people most affected by change that we can actually meet those challenges head on. Want to understand the nature of our evolving labour market? Talking to the *AFR* or the *Economist* alone won't help, you will need also to ask a worker on a casual contract for her experiences. Want to know about the realities of climate change? Neither the executives of large companies nor environmental scientists alone can suffice; we need to talk with a family living without air conditioning in Western Sydney. Want to appreciate the changing nature of globalised migration? You can't do better than to listen to a refuge child locked away for years on end in Manus.

I do not mean this glibly. I believe that the extraordinary power of the everyday is needed now more than ever because of the extraordinary danger of the moment we are in. Putting that another way: it is the lived experience of those people who are grappling with the systemic failings that we currently face that offer the crucial beginnings of a plausible politics of change. And, at the moment, their perspective is usually missing from any effort to redress those failings.

This a powerful rebuke to the ways in which things are currently run. But it is not just a rebuke. It is a powerful, practical program that has the chance of making a reality of Norman's ideal. There are real opportunities to change political decision-making so that it is genuinely open to the experiences of the everyday right now. The change that we need to make if we are going to succeed has three parts to it. Some of which we can *call* for, some of which we can *start* ourselves.

First, it means opening up the formal processes of politics. The secrecy of the party room must be gone forever. Party selections should be opened up to participants of all backgrounds. And more than that, power must be devolved closer to the people whose lives it affects. There is no reason why the elected officials of the Commonwealth and the States, or the experts of the Productivity Commissions, should enjoy the monopoly of privileges that they currently have. Australia needs real vibrant, city government, proper neighbourhood representation. Power must reside at the lowest possible level if it is going to be responsive to the people whose voices really count.

So, opening up power is where it must all begin. But it doesn't end there. Because, second, it also means doing all we can to equip as many people as possible from as diverse a range of backgrounds as possible with the skills and opportunities to exercise genuine political influence. Power is not just about formal opportunities; it is about having the real ability to grasp them. What could that mean in practice? Schools could teach 'action civics' to give children a real-life experience of finding their voice and sharpening their influence while they are young. NGOs and peak bodies should provide new opportunities for so-called 'service recipients' or 'end-users' to become genuinely equal participants in the day-to-day governance of their own lives. And great universities should play their part in making our world-leading research and expertise freely available to those who need it. That way those who do not currently enjoy privileged access can make a far better case for the change they want to see in their lives, taking on the established authorities from a more equal starting point.

So—first, opening up formal power, and second, equipping people with the skills and information they need to be able to use it. But that's still not all. Third, and perhaps most importantly, we must all do what we can to protect the truly open and democratic spaces we currently do have in Australia. And expand them for the future. Where are those spaces? Well, think of it this way: Most of us didn't learn how to be an active citizen in campaign groups or on the picket lines. We learnt it through everyday experience. As the political theorist, Bonnie Honig, puts it: "The democratic experiment involves living cheek by jowl with others. Sharing classrooms, roads, and buses."[1]

Just reflect on that for a moment. Where did you last have a conversation with someone whose point of view was very different from your own? Someone whose background was vastly different? I am pretty sure it wasn't in an 'officially' political space. It was somewhere else. And the market cannot provide all the answers here either. In the United Kingdom, it used to happen in the doctor's waiting room. One of the reasons British people are obsessed with the National Health Service, has nothing to do with health in itself—in fact, its record on health is fairly mixed—but has everything to do with this shared experience. When I was growing up, that waiting room was the one space where you would see all of the village—rich and poor, young and old, disabled and not disabled, migrant and local. There was no division there. People talked to each other. Laughed, complained, argued occasionally, mourned when they had to. And it is not just the NHS that can do that. Any society can as long as it has museums, libraries, public transport, open public spaces, campuses upon which we feel welcome, buildings in which we feel safe and secure. In other words, any society in which we learn the realities of coming together despite our differences. Simply by living. And yet—and here's the rub—too often those spaces are in retreat right now, undermined by the rise of digital technologies and the intensification of commercial pressures on the public realm.

Jesse Norman teaches us that the "moral basis of commercial society lies in the ceaseless exchange of mutual obligations and personal regard." That is true not just of commercial societies but of all decent societies. But in Australia and other established democracies, the preconditions of that spirit are ebbing away. People feel overlooked, powerless, and disconnected. At the moment, our politics currently offers little way out. Instead, it falls foul of precisely the extremes that Lawrence and others saw in the early decades of the last century, blighted by denial and purism. But it doesn't have to be like that. Our mission, inspired by Jesse Norman's words, should be to come together over party lines and independent of ideological allegiance to build an alternative politics; one that treasures the wisdom of everyday life as Burke and Smith did, by opening up power, ensuring everyone has voice, and that we can meet together in the public square.

2

BURKE VS SMITH

ON NATURAL LAW, SOCIAL ORDER AND SYMPATHY

ADRIAN PABST

Conservatism is electorally successful but intellectually in disarray. Both Brexit and the victory of Donald Trump are symptoms of a profound crisis of meaning and leadership that also besets Australia's Liberal Party. Margaret Thatcher, Ronald Reagan, and John Howard held together the tensions between the economic liberalism of the New Right and the traditional, patriotic conservatism of the older right. But since then conservative parties have seen the dominance of economic liberals and the rise of right-wing libertarians. Both seek solace in abstraction from human embeddedness in relationships and institutions. And both marginalised the 'compassionate conservatism' that tries to conserve the values, traditions, and ways of life which constitute a shared national community. Liberalism and libertarianism deracinate once-great parties from the everyday existence of people, hollowing out civic institutions and public services in the name of individual choice and freedom from the constricting shackles of government. Whether Boris Johnson's victory reflects a tactical shift or brings about a permanent realignment remains to be seen. What is in question is the ethos of conservatism with a deeper story of mutual obligations and national renewal anchored in a sense of the common good.

It is this narrative that Jesse Norman has retrieved and retold with great intellectual vigour in his writings—from his early work on the political philosopher Michael Oakeshott to his essay on 'Compassionate Conservatism', from his pamphlet critiquing cartel capitalism to his essay on 'Compassionate Economics' and his tome *The Big Society*, from his celebrated study on Edmund Burke to his recent book about Adam Smith.[1] Norman's special talent is to combine a compelling critique of un-conservative philosophies and ideological traditions with a rediscovery of the sources of conservatism, notably an Aristotelian sense of the human condition and Burke's civic covenant as the foundation of a democratic politics.

His 2018 PM Glynn Lecture is an elegant synthesis and development of his important ideas. If, as Norman observes, the centre-ground of Western politics has collapsed and is now a void filled by radical-right or far-left extremes, the question confronting the West is about much more than the discontents of contemporary capitalism. It is about the "nature of modern society" and the pre-political "we" on which a common life depends—one that involves a degree of loyalty, duty, and sacrifice. How in our age of anger are we to recreate a sense of shared belonging to national communities? Can we re-build a polity around mutual obligations binding together neighbourhoods and nations?

Norman is right to doubt whether the four dominant modern approaches to these questions—natural law, social contract, Kantian duty, and utilitarian ethics—can provide adequate answers.

Therefore, he proposes a fifth approach that he claims can help us to find ways out of the current impasse. He defines this approach as the "tradition of natural utility", which he traces to the works of Burke and Smith. This tradition is supposed to do three things: (1) to draw out the complementarity of Burke and Smith as the joint pioneers of an alternative modernity; (2) to show how their legacy avoids the limits of natural law, social contract, Kant, and utilitarianism and provides an enduring vision of society; (3) to reclaim the political centre-ground based on a renewed conservatism capable of replacing the predations of the capitalist system with the moral basis of commercial society.

However, the idea of 'natural utility' is less a living tradition than an intellectual invention that, to my mind, has three main shortcomings. First of all, the tradition of natural utility is meant to synthesise Burke and Smith, but there are more significant differences in their respective conceptions of social order and sympathy than Norman recognises. Secondly, the idea of natural utility is meant to avoid the assumption about a transcendent God or nature on which the tradition of natural law rests, but Burke's political philosophy is much more indebted to certain conceptions of natural law than Norman acknowledges. Thirdly, Smith's idea of commercial society has both philosophical and political problems, which suggest that Norman's interpretation is unworkable as a solution to the crisis of conservatism and the collapse of the political centre.

I will begin with Norman's reading of Burke and Smith. Burke has bequeathed to us a vision of society grounded in human experience, not abstract principles—a social order that evolves gradually and is built around intermediary institutions formed by social interaction. These institutions, Norman writes, "are ultimately grounded in feeling and emotion, which guide and direct man's reason. They are bound together by affection, identity and interest". The social order is an inheritance, which imposes obligations on each generation to preserve, possibly enhance, and pass on inherited institutions and practices to the next generation. That is why in the *Reflections on the Revolution in France* Burke defines society as "a partnership not only between those who are living, but between those who are living, those who are dead, and those who are to be born".[2]

While Burke outlines an overarching vision, Smith elucidates its inner workings. For Norman, Smith's notion of 'commercial society' suggests that we improve our lot and become more fully human through processes of exchange that are both economic and ethical. As social beings, humans exchange not only goods and services but also regard and admiration. Key to Smith's moral philosophy and political economy is his account of sympathy and the creation of mutual obligations based on social interaction. Empathy with others and recognition of their talents and achievements create the conditions for norms that govern both personal and social behaviour. As Norman puts it succinctly, "fact leads to values via norms".

Thus, Smith and Burke would seem to complement each other. The exchange of mutual obligations and personal regard becomes the basis of commercial society with moral markets at its heart. The ethical norms generated in this process form habits, practices, and institutions which favour representative government. Taken together, their conception of social order gives rise to a moderate modernity of human advancement rooted in tradition: "As Burke is the hinge of our political modernity, so is Smith the hinge of our economic, and in many ways our social, modernity. Theirs are momentous achievements".

Much of this story is persuasive, especially the emphasis on man as a social animal whose nature is to be in society—a conception that contrasts with Hobbes's asocial state of nature or Rousseau's conception of pre-social liberty. However, Norman dismisses the tradition of natural law perhaps too hastily and he glosses over the role of divine natural law in Burke, which is closely connected to his conception of virtue ethics. As a 'philosopher in action', Burke argued that human nature, like politics, is a question of balance between virtue and vice because humans are capable of both good and evil. As human beings are neither perfect nor totally depraved, the role of institutions is to encourage virtue and to limit vice.

Prudence is the "first of all virtues" and "the God of this lower world".[3] Unlike abstract moral precepts (as in Rousseau or Kant), virtues are universal principles that are embodied in particular practices. For Burke, the "principled practice" of prudence applies as much to relations among individuals within a single society as it does to the relations between countries within what he calls "commonwealths of culture".[4] The idea of social order extends to the international society of nations and peoples.

What links Burke's conception of humans as social beings to his account of justice as the principle that organizes relations within the social order is his invocation of natural law. In his speeches on the impeachment of Warren Hastings, he insists that there is no such thing as arbitrary power because it is not human will which determines legitimacy, but instead eternal law: "we are all born in subjection—all born equally, high and low, governors and governed, in subjection to one great, immutable, preexistent law . . . by which we are knit and connected in the eternal frame of the universe". Since this law is a gift from God in whom will and reason are the same, it follows for Burke that the authority by which men rule over others is governed by "the eternal laws of Him that gave it, with which no human authority can dispense". These "eternal laws of justice, to which we are all subject", provide the foundations for "the laws of morality [that] are the same everywhere".[5] Particular practices and specific institutions mediate universal principles of ethics that transcend purely human standards. Otherwise we would be condemned to choose between theocratic absolutism or the revolutionary violence of mob rule.

Scholars like Michael Freeman and R. J. Vincent contend that references to God in Burke are less a reflection of philosophy than a function of sociology. Freeman's argument is that Burke's reliance on religion has more to do with social utility than Christian metaphysics.[6] In the words of Vincent, "the legitimacy derived from this [God's] delegation provided the reason for social solidarity instructing the habit of co-operation. But it was in the habitual end of this connection that Burke was chiefly interested: he was a sociologist of religion before he was a theologian".[7]

However, such interpretations are incompatible with Burke's repeated appeals to God throughout his writings. Human beings, despite the Fall and the irruption of evil and sin, are capable of discovering natural law because it has been mediated in history through living traditions of knowledge instantiated in practices. Given Burke's distrust of purely human reason and abstract principles, these traditions of knowledge cannot be purely man-made.

As social beings, "we know, and what is better, we feel inwardly that religion is the basis of civil society and the source of all good and of all comfort".[8] For Burke, God is the ultimate source of our being and our capacity for moral action: "If there be a God such as we conceive, he must be our Maker. If he is our Maker, there is a Relation between us. If there be a Relation between us some Duty must arise from that Relation, since we cannot conceive that a reasonable Creature can be placed in any Relation that does not give rise to some Duty".[9]

Far from serving a merely sociological function, Burke's references to divine natural law are central to his conception of politics[10]—a covenant between humanity and its Creator that is dimly reflected in covenantal relations among the generations of each nation and between the nations forming a commonwealth. As Burke writes,

> We have obligations to mankind at large, which are not in

consequence of any special voluntary pact. They arise from the relation of man to man, and the relation of man to God, which relations are not matters of pact. On the contrary, the force of all pacts which we enter into with any particular person or number of persons, amongst mankind, depends upon these prior obligations.[11]

In turn, mutual obligations based on natural law imply that human beings are naturally linked to fellow human beings by bonds of sympathy. Together with the passions of imitation and ambition, sympathy helps to produce a social order that is not imposed upon some pre-existing chaos, but rather emerges from nature by fusing a concern for others (sympathy) with following the example (imitation) of those who excel and can offer virtuous leadership (ambition). Although they are "of a complicated kind", these three passions "branch out into a variety of forms agreeable to that variety of ends they are to serve in the great chain of society".[12]

Whatever the disagreement about natural law, there is no doubt that Norman's reading of Burke rightly highlights his "indomitable belief in ordered liberty, and in the right of humans to live their lives well and to enjoy the benefits of human society". What makes Burke so important for contemporary politics is his profound philosophical critique of political rationalism and of revolutionary idealism, as well as the development of a political method rooted in time and place—in particular history and specific circumstances instead of theoretical absolutism (as in Kant and Rousseau). The reason why Burke remains central to a renewal of conservatism today is because, as Norman writes, he is the "first modern philosopher to treat the idea of society as a basic category within politics".[13]

I am less persuaded, however, by Norman's argument that Adam Smith's social philosophy complements Burke's political philosophy. My main point of contention is the meaning of sympathy in Smith and his conception of social order. It is true, as

Norman suggests, that in Smith's political economy markets are embedded in networks of social sympathy, but this embedding is limited by a double distrust. First of all, his distrust of the human ability to extend virtue beyond the 'thick ties' of family relations and friendship. As Smith himself argues, "Men, though naturally sympathetic, feel so little for one another, with whom they have no particular connection, in comparison of what they feel for themselves; the misery of one, who is merely their fellow-creature, is of so little importance to them in comparison even of a small inconveniency of their own".[14]

Secondly, Smith's distrust of human association, which he claims nearly always leads to the vice of corruption. This claim underpins his critique of intermediary institutions in a famous passage in the *Wealth of Nations*:

> People of the same trade seldom meet together, even for merriment and diversion, but the conversation ends in a conspiracy against the public, or in some contrivance to raise prices. . . But though the law cannot hinder people of the same trade from sometimes assembling together, it ought to do nothing to facilitate such assemblies; much less to render them necessary.[15]

By contrast with Burke, sympathetic ties for Smith are confined to a resonance with the other person's private needs and feelings and have nothing to do with the co-shaping of a shared sensibility. Therefore, the Glaswegian professor did not allow 'sympathies' to enter into the economic contract itself. The Italian economist-philosophers Luigino Bruni and Stefano Zamagni rightly argue that, for Smith, "*the market* itself doesn't require them, and works even better without them (hence the praise of weak ties)".[16] Smith's notion of "cooperation without benevolence" negatively links his moral philosophy in the *Theory of Moral Sentiments* to his political economy in the *Wealth of Nations*, and the outcome is a conception of moral markets without strong social virtues.

In other words, the more tacit economic contract conceived by

Smith is by no means the substantive, shared traditional horizon envisaged by Burke. Rather, it is a more dispersed and diversified version of the harmonious balancing of rival self-interest akin to the social contract model. Smith and his friend David Hume do not allow sympathetic concerns to function as drivers of market processes. In this respect, they can be contrasted with other currents of Scottish social thought, exemplified by Dugald Stewart and later Thomas Reid, who were far less convinced that economic motivations and concerns for 'justice' were based on negative fear, and granted a much greater role to a shared 'common sense' of 'public utility', still underwritten by divine natural law.[17]

Thus, the crucial difference between Burke and Smith is that the former views markets (and states) as embedded in social relations, whereas the latter considers market relations as the basis rather than the outcome of human sociability. Smith himself puts this as follows:

> Society may subsist among different men, as among different merchants, from a sense of its utility, without any mutual love or affection; and though no man in it should owe any obligation, or be bound in gratitude to any other, it may still be upheld by a mercenary exchange of good offices according to an agreed valuation.[18]

Of course, Norman is right that Smith was no advocate of capitalism. On the contrary, he desired a market with few monopolies, modest prices, high wages, a vocational not a functional (factory-like) division of labour, and one that tended to return more people to work in the countryside. This almost 'ecological' factor in his thinking was driven by his insistence that a healthy economy puts real concrete wealth before notional abstract wealth, and that the most basic of all wealth is human food. A renewed political economy should critically embrace such objectives and reclaim Smith from both right-wing caricatures of him as a precursor of neoliberal market fundamentalism, and left-wing misconstruals of him as a proto-Keynesian social-democrat (as in the work of

Emma Rothschild and Amartya Sen, among others).[19] He by no means thought that market equilibrium always occurs automatically, and therefore considered that it has to be constantly shaped by state intervention.

However, to some extent Smith's notion of cooperation between the 'invisible' and the 'visible' hand did anticipate neo-classical economics. One could even say that, in certain respects, he relied too much on public intervention and did not allow for any direct relational and reciprocal interpersonal role in securing prosperity. Instead, Smith's moral markets without strong virtues privilege the economic and the political over the social—the 'invisible hand' of the market and the 'visible hand' of the state over the sympathetic ties binding together society.

Norman's lessons from Smith provide a compelling corrective to the liberal and libertarian takeover of contemporary conservatism. But faced with the deep distrust of political institutions as well as oligarchic concentrations of power and wealth, the danger is that Smith's commercial society retains the focus primarily on the state and the market, which are (seen to be) dominated by impersonal forces. Burke's legacy, by contrast, shifts the emphasis to what makes us human and what makes society social—our irreducible relationality and a partnership between past, present, and future generations rather than exchange in the 'here and now'. Norman's reading of Burke charts a path towards a renewal of conservatism based on a politics of virtue.[20] For it is the strong social virtues of generosity, loyalty, and duty that nurture the way we live in society.

Burke's legacy is also more useful in solving current political problems than Smith's. Appeals to the abstract ideals of liberty and equality ring hollow. They overlook the relationships with our family, friends or fellow citizens, which embody principles in practices. That is why Burke rejected the possessive individualism of liberal thinking in favour of social freedom. True liberty is secured by what he called "equality of restraint", not empty free choice. Freedom and equality require lived fraternity among citizens who have common needs, and fraternity is largely absent from Smith. But the dominant political traditions, including conservatism, have abandoned any sense of interpersonal solidarity. They have instead embraced the impersonal forces of central state control and atomised market exchange that undermine society.

The collusion of state and market in dispossessing people is something Burke conceptualised more than 200 years ago. The French Revolution did not simply involve terror. It also gave rise to capitalism in France based on expropriation, speculation, and dispossession. First the revolutionaries converted the confiscated property of the crown and the church into money, which was lent to the state. The money became public debt contracted by the government to wage war. This created a new class of 'monied interest' that charged usurious interest rates, making money out of money and generating speculative profits. Then the state taxed the people and robbed them of their assets to service the growing mountain of public debt financed by private creditors. State agents and private speculators formed what Burke described as an "ignoble oligarchy", which applies to banking conglomerates and the global tech platforms today.[21]

What this shows is that the capitalist system does not primarily substitute one set of property relationships or one dominant class for another. Then as now, capitalism is driven by speculative capital. It ends up dissolving real value into nominal wealth because it is disconnected from production of value or shared ownership. Burke called this "paper-money despotism", and our economic model built on debt and easy credit bears a certain resemblance to it. The task is to civilise capitalism and turn it into a social market embedded in institutions and relationships governed by sympathetic ties of solidarity.

There are other lessons from Burke's political economy. His

emphasis on covenantal ties among generations can help us think through the growing economic injustice between young and old today. Burke's conception of society as a partnership provides a radical middle-ground between individualism and collectivism by balancing individual rights with mutual obligations and contributions with rewards. Yet today we have a culture of entitlement that does just the opposite. Workers who have contributed a lifetime receive 'nothing for something'—the same meagre jobseekers' allowance as the young or migrants who get 'something for nothing'. Justice without compassion is empty, just as compassion without justice is blind. The path towards greater economic justice involves a renewed balance of interests among the generations and the building of a common good between estranged sections of society.

Covenants endow social ties with meaning that is missing from the social contract tradition and tends to be underplayed by Smith's philosophy. By contrast, Burke emphasises the irreducible relationality of humans that underpins reciprocal relations. We are born into social relationships, "the little platoon we belong to in society", and these are the first object of our affections. We learn to love and care for family, neighbours and friends. This love creates a sense of attachment and belonging that extends to our fellow citizens and humankind—the strangers in our midst who become part of our communities.

Contemporary politics has little to say about our social nature. We are embodied beings who are embedded in relationships and institutions. They command affection and forge attachment as they are rooted in people's identity and interests. These "public affections", as Burke called them, are indispensable to the good functioning of the rule of law. They build trust and cooperation which cannot be mandated by rules or regulations. Going beyond social capital and even the exchange of esteem, Burke's emphasis on affective attachment captures something fundamental about our human nature, which the philosopher Mary Midgley puts well:

> the reality of affectionate bonds among social animals is now fully documented by ethnologists. Their sociability is not just a means to an end. . . Of course this affection does not mean that they love each other unconditionally. . . They will in many circumstances compete with and attack each other. But they do all this against a wider background of mutual emotional dependency and friendly acceptance.[22]

Far from being just an appeal to sentiment, Burke's conception of affective attachment shifts the focus to the 'principled practice' of mutual recognition based on human relationality upon which a prosperous market economy and a vibrant democracy depend. Burke's appeal to love and friendship reflects the Aristotelian primacy of relationships over impersonal mechanisms. The practice of lived fraternity can shape a politics of affective attachment to people, place, and purpose.

3

Burke and Australian Britishness

Gregory Melleuish

It is interesting that of the two key figures who are meant to be the inspiration for the contemporary Liberal Party of Australia, John Stuart Mill and Edmund Burke, it is much easier to trace the influence of Mill than Burke.[1] Mill was the great icon of nineteenth-century English liberalism and the colonies revered him. David Kemp has recently emphasised the influence of Mill as a liberal thinker for Australia in the nineteenth century.[2]

However, we should always recognise that the invocation of a name does not always mean that the ideas of the person bearing that name have necessarily had an impact on those invoking it. This is especially the case in a country such as Australia that has not had a particularly well-developed public culture in which ideas are discussed in great depth. Rather, one could say that certain ideas drift into the political culture and are absorbed by it in an almost unconscious fashion.

Australians have long valued freedom and seen it as a defining quality of their way of life. This does not mean, however, that they are advocates of some abstract ideal of 'liberty' such as animates their American cousins. In the eighteenth century, North Americans largely understood their freedoms and liberties in terms of their rights as Englishmen. The revolution changed this view; it discredited the British connection and the Americans could only view the British as conspiring against their rights and seeking to enslave them. Rights then must be universal in nature, although, given that the Americans did not recognise the rights of their slaves, this strategy was perhaps more rhetorical than actual.

Unlike the Americans, or the French, Australians did not have to confront the issue of universal rights. Australia remains the only country of English British origins not to have created some sort of bill of rights. As James Allan has argued, Australia remains the last Anglo-Saxon common law democracy in which the law and parliament are the primary defenders of rights as opposed to some sort of bill of rights that transfers control of such rights from the parliament to the judiciary.[3] The Commonwealth Constitution does not have a bill of rights, nor did its framers consider that something such as natural law was part of its foundation.[4]

The legacy of Burke in Australia is not something to be judged by the influence of Burke's ideas on particular thinkers and political figures. Until recently, few individuals in Australia readily identified as conservatives, let alone as 'Burkeans'. The influence of Burkean political ideas was significant in Australia but it was not so much at a conscious intellectual level as a process of osmosis as the British in Australia absorbed those political ideas that they found to be most compatible. At first sight, this appears to be a matter of astonishment, as one would normally expect that the members of a colony far from the metropolitan culture would adopt a primarily rationalist approach to political matters. After all, they had no option but to construct new political orders, and to create written constitutions, something lacking in Britain. They had to codify that which the British were happy to leave as custom and convention.

Australians have rarely identified as conservatives. Attempts to put in place some sort of Tory hierarchical order in New South Wales in the 1820s came to nothing. As argued by Stuart Piggin and Bob Linder, the British in the Australian colonies remained resolutely Whig and liberal in their politics and largely Evangelical in their religion.[5] Even the advocates of a colonial aristocracy, such as W. C. Wentworth and James Macarthur, were essentially Whigs. Piggin, Linder, and Kemp demonstrate that the Australian colonists were advocates of what Jesse Norman has described as 'natural utility', a utility that sat easily with both Evangelical religion and the traditions of British constitutionalism. It was, therefore, an understanding of natural utility, as shall be seen, that was embedded in the colonists' self-understanding of themselves as being British.

Placing to one side the issue of the Indigenous inhabitants, in the peculiar circumstances of the Australian colonies there was no downtrodden rural underclass. Even before the introduction of universal manhood suffrage most adult males in the colonies would have qualified to vote using English criteria.[6] Catherine Helen Spence noted the difference between the prosperous conditions of the ordinary person in South Australia and the poor living conditions of the rural poor when visiting the land of her birth, Scotland, in the 1860s.[7]

Despite their strange origin as a prison, the Australian colonies were born liberal. They were, as David Malouf argues, the product of the late eighteenth-century British Enlightenment with its emphasis on reasonableness and utility,[8] and buttressed by a religion that emphasised both spirituality and a duty to engage with the world. The Australian colonies were a particular type of British/English society, similar to the homeland but at the same time distinctive and different. Burke understood the reality that colonial societies were different from those of the metropolitan culture, but not that different:

> This Character of the Americans, a love of Freedom is the predominating feature which marks and distinguishes the whole: and as an ardent is always a jealous affection, your Colonies become suspicious, restive, and untractable, whenever they see the least attempt to wrest from them by force, or shuffle from them by chicane, what they think the only advantage worth living for. This fierce spirit of Liberty is stronger in the English Colonies probably than in any other people of the earth; and this from a great variety of powerful causes; which, to understand the true temper of their minds, and the direction which this spirit takes, it will not be amiss to lay open somewhat more largely.
>
> First, the people of the Colonies are descendants of Englishmen. England, Sir, is a nation, which still I hope respects, and formerly adored, her freedom. The Colonists emigrated from you when this part of your character was most predominant; and they took this bias and direction the moment they parted from your hands. They are therefore not only devoted to Liberty, but to Liberty according to English ideas, and on English principles. Abstract Liberty, like other mere abstractions, is not to be found. Liberty inheres in some sensible object; and every nation has formed to itself some favourite point, which by way of eminence becomes the criterion of their happiness.[9]

It is clear that the Australian colonists were not as fractious as were their American cousins—the Eureka Stockade pales into insignificance when compared to the American Revolution—but this does not mean that they were not also lovers of liberty. Given the opportunity, they were happy to fight for their liberty, be it for the introduction of trial by jury or for the end of the transportation of convicts to the colonies. Australian colonists could complain against the evils of rule from 'Downing Street' just as the Americans had in the previous century:

> But what can Downing street do? Well: It can turn upside down the policy of years, without moving "the House;" it can dismiss the most faithful servant of the Crown, without a paragraph ap-

pearing in the *Times*; it can cripple colonial commerce and kindle colonial resentment; hundreds may be ruined, and thousands made disloyal; and not an angry word be heard, not a window be broken in Downing-street itself. It can support with obstinacy the despotism of the governor, and the incompetence of the judge; it can force upon a feeble colony the burdens of pauperism and crime; it can multiply offices, and make them the reward of political subservience; and not until some great event imposes restriction upon its power, has any great party ever been found to question or suppress its abuses.[10]

Despite Burke's protestations, the British government of the 1770s seemed to be incapable of working out an imperial arrangement that would work to the satisfaction of both the Americans and the British. Considering the case of Ireland, it appears that the same obstinacy that governed the British regarding eighteenth-century America continued down until the twentieth century, which may be why Brexit has become such an intractable problem.

The case of the more distant settler societies was an entirely different case as Canada, Australia, and New Zealand were granted what was known as responsible government, or sometimes 'party government'. 'Downing Street' willingly allowed its colonies the right to run their own internal affairs, including financial responsibility. In the Australian case, initially the governor had the right to refuse legislation or to refer it to the British government, but over time that control diminished.[11] Of course, when the Australian colonies federated, they required an Act passed by the Westminster Parliament. Fear of British involvement affected the way in which the Commonwealth Parliament approached the matter of immigration restriction.

Even allowing for the fact that the colonial governments did not have total control over their affairs, the reality was that these governments, in most matters, could largely do as they pleased. This model of empire indicates that, in these cases at least, the

British government had come to appreciate that Burke had been correct in the 1770s and that there was more to be gained from what we would now term 'soft power' when dealing with overseas British communities than from the use of coercive measures. It meant that Australia and New Zealand would remain tenaciously loyal to the 'mother country' for the next century.

In the absence of coercive practices, what came to tie Australia and Britain together were bonds of a much more informal nature that emphasised ties based on common feeling and values. Australians understood themselves to be British, even to be more British than the British themselves. Hence, there was the famous claim that Australians are 98 percent British.[12] Labor Prime Ministers of Irish descent happily claimed the British heritage and Australians made sacrifices to send food to Britain in the years after World War II.[13]

What this meant is that Australians never felt the need to step outside of their British heritage to understand and explain their politics. That heritage remained foundational; there was no need to refer to universal political principles or to invoke universal human rights. For the drafters of the Commonwealth Constitution, the British constitution was pivotal. It was simply the best in world.[14] As part of 'Greater Britain', it was as much an element of their inheritance as it was of those living in Britain.[15]

The Australian colonies subscribed to a cult of 'Britishness' as part of their fundamental identity. This Britishness had both a religious and a civic dimension. In the nineteenth century, in particular, to be British meant to be Protestant. Evangelicalism was fundamental to the values that animated the Australian colonists in both their social and political concerns. It is no accident that the decline of Britishness in Australia has been accompanied by the secularisation, or more properly dechristianisation of its Protestant population.

Cocooned within their Britishness, the Australian colonists

adapted a set of attitudes and values that can rightfully be described as Burkean. They did view the basis of their liberties and freedoms to lie not in natural and universal rights but in the British tradition that they had inherited. They were free because they were British; to remain free they had to remain British. This has had some very important long-term effects, one of which is that many Australians are still very suspicious about expressing their rights in universal terms.

It is difficult to say the extent to which the writings of Burke shaped this political culture as opposed to the way in which Australians absorbed political ideals from Britain that Burke had helped to shape. Certainly, colonial political culture was decidedly liberal in outlook, and the colonists looked to Gladstone as an exemplar.[16]

Although the colonists could equally set up John Stuart Mill as a liberal paragon, it is doubtful that they fully appreciated the implications of many of Mill's ideas. Their notion of liberty was framed from within what might be termed a British cultural understanding. This framing used a large number of assumptions regarding the British character and the role that the British were playing in spreading science, knowledge, and peace into all corners of the earth.[17] The British, including the English, were, according to this vision, a practical people who sought real solutions to real problems. Hence, they would have appreciated J. H. Newman's assessment of Hurrell Froude that "he was an Englishman to the backbone in his severe adherence to the real and the concrete" and applied it to themselves.[18]

Their understanding of politics was real and concrete, embedded in a lived reality. The first British colony in Australia may have been established as a gaol but it was no gulag. It remained a society in which the rights of free-born Englishmen had not been extinguished and which would be reinstated, with a bit of struggle involved, when circumstances improved. The combination of the liberalism of the late Enlightenment and Evangelicalism came together to help mould a political culture that valued liberty, but it was the liberty of free British Protestants. Of course, Catholics could be accommodated within this liberal order, albeit with a certain degree of difficulty. Sectarianism reared its ugly head despite the best of intentions. What had no place was a Tory High Church vision of society based on traditional ideas of hierarchy.

The Australian colonists created the sort of political order of which Burke would have readily approved as it sought to claim its freedom as an inheritance. It is one of those accidents of history that it was another Burke, Governor Richard Bourke, who did so much to lay the foundations of a liberal order through his educational policies.[19] The Australian political order would be liberal because, as with the American colonists prior to 1776, they claimed their liberties as free Britons.

Nevertheless, this did not mean that it was possible to translate the British constitution into Australia. They sought to re-shape the British political order to fit their peculiar circumstances. On some matters, however, they had no choice but to innovate. For example, if they were going to have two houses of parliament, what was to be the basis of the selection of the upper house? They wanted two houses but had no desire for an aristocracy. They tried a number of options, including nomination, as in New South Wales, and election by a limited franchise as in Victoria.[20] When they federated, the obvious solution presented itself; the Senate would be the States' house.

There were other adjustments, but still in the Burkean mode. The granting of responsible government in the 1850s, created the expectation that the political system would take the form of 'party government' along the English lines. After all, the model presumed the existence of some sort of party to provide support for the government. Again, this follows from Burke's view of party as a legitimate element of a political system. For Burke, differences in political outlook do not lead to 'rage of party' and, in opposition to Bolingbroke,* a properly functioning British constitution does not mean the eradication of party differences.[21]

Unfortunately, the dominance of liberalism in the colonies prevented the immediate creation of a party system as there were very few conservatives. This did not prevent a diversity of political views in the colonies, nor was there any attempt to impose a uniform political outlook. Parties simply took some time to emerge, which they had by the 1890s. Responsible government eventually came to mean party government.

Even when it came to the issue of creating a constitution that would enable the various colonies to federate, it was clear that what animated them was the desire to remain as true to the spirit of the British constitution as possible as can be seen in this quote from the radical liberal Alfred Deakin:

> I take it that we may remit this bill to our constituents with some confidence, since it is a natural outgrowth of the constitutions already existing in Australia, of which we ourselves have had experience, striking its roots back to that British Constitution from which the free institutions of our race have sprung. It does not present the same features as the constitution of the mother country, nor yet is it identical, by any means, with any single constitution which can be found in Australia; but it ought to be a source of confidence to note that it has proceeded on the same well-grounded lines and well proved methods which have received the sanction of our people in all these colonies. This constitution will not present itself to them as something strange, foreign, or abnormal; but as something which their own experience will have prepared them to understand and appreciate. The work of our hands, although it will bear traces of the study of the constitutions of the Unit-

---

* Bolingbroke believed that the Glorious Revolution of 1688 had restored the ancient constitution of England. In so doing it removed the need for parties because in a properly functioning constitution there was no basis for political division. Parties, therefore, become factions that conspire against the public good, as Bolingbroke saw to be the case with the Walpole Whigs. See, in particular, his *A Dissertation on Parties* (Cadell, 1736).

ed States and of Canada, and of constitutions even more remote, is yet distinctly an Anglo-Saxon, saturated through and through with the spirit and confidence of self-government, which has been characteristic of the race.[22]

As Chavura and I have argued elsewhere, Burkean themes permeated the debates of the constitutional conventions of the 1890s.[23] The delegates to the various conventions were determined to stay as close to the 'spirit' of the British constitution as possible, to innovate as little as possible, and were decidedly against attempts to use abstract theory as the basis of the Constitution. Ironically, the Constitution's one genuine innovation for which there was no precedent, the nexus between the two houses of parliament, is perhaps one of the genuine failures of the drafters.[24]

In another area, that of the nature of representation, one can see the direct influence of Burke. Colonial politicians understood themselves to be trustees and not delegates.[25] Many of them may have been 'roads and bridges' members, but they professed not to be acting under instructions from those who elected them. They acted as independent agents who consulted their consciences on what was best for the community. This may seem to be somewhat in conflict with the idea of 'party' but it should be understood that that party in the nineteenth century did not mean the rigid machine that it has become today.

The big challenge came with the rise of the Australian Labor Party, which did view its members of parliament as delegates, but delegates who obeyed the dictates of the party. This created a chasm between it and those claiming to be liberals, not least because it undermined the principles of responsible government by making Labor members responsible to the party. Judith Brett has argued that this chasm was crucial in the way in which the Australian party system constituted itself after 1909.[26]

Did this mean that the Labor Party had ceased to live in a

Burkean world? The answer to this would be no. The Labor Party retained its great faith in parliamentary practice and in the principles of responsible government. This included the idea that responsible government meant party government, and that parties were a crucial element of parliamentary democracy. Hence a Labor leader of the early 1960s, Arthur Calwell, could quote "with some pleasure" Burke's defence of parties from *Thoughts on the Present Discontents*.[27]

Considered in a different light, the adoption of the delegate model of representation proved Burke's views on theoretical political models as it was to be the source of many of the woes of the Labor Party over the course of the twentieth century.[28]

Labor and non-Labor alike accepted that the ideal form of political system for Australia, as a part of greater Britain, was the British system of responsible government, even if in the Australian context responsible government encased itself in a federal structure. Both sides of politics knew that there were rules and conventions to be followed, rules and conventions that were part of their British inheritance. This was reinforced by a very strong sentiment that the British were the kin of Australians.

Both sides of politics in Australia were for a very long time constitutionally conservative, even if they proposed social policies that were not. As has been noted, this was true of Alfred Deakin who sounds very much like a Burkean during the constitutional conventions, even if he proposed quite liberal innovative measures during his time as prime minister. The same was largely true of the Labor Party. True, they would have liked to have abolished the States and the Senate, but only because they believed so strongly in responsible government as the foundation of Australian democracy. If either party wished the Commonwealth to assume extra powers they attempted to do so through the formal mechanism of the referendum. They were rulebound and had an expectation that the established rules be followed, be they written down or in the form of constitutional conventions. This is why the events of 1975, when first the Senate refused supply and then the Governor-General sacked the prime minister, came as such a shock to the Labor Party. There had somehow been a subversion of the understood rules.

The high priest of Englishness, and of Burkean sentiment in Australia, was Sir Robert Menzies. Menzies always understood himself as a liberal, never as a conservative or Tory. His instincts, like those of Burke, were Whiggish, seeking a proper balance between stability and change, but always with a desire to preserve liberty. That is why he wrote about the "art of politics"; an art that he believed that the English had developed so admirably.[29] With men such as Curtin, Chifley, and Menzies at the helm, Australia felt secure in its British and Burkean heritage until the 1960s. Their respect for the traditions of parliamentary government was instinctive and in no need of being submitted to the scrutiny of 'theory'.

Two things have happened since the 1960s:

- The instinctive Burkean quality of Australian politics has declined in tandem with the decline of Britishness in Australia. The events of 1975 were emblematic of this transformation. The written Constitution has become more important and along with it has emerged a more rationalist approach to politics.[30]

- With political changes that have occurred in the country, the early Burke, with whom Australians had much instinctive sympathy has become less important in Australian political culture while the Burke of the *Reflections on the Revolution in France*, a much more ideologically strident Burke, has emerged in his place. Burke has become a much more ideologically conservative figure.

In other words, as the nature of politics in Australia has transformed itself in recent years, so has the place of Burke in Australian political culture. For example, as the Labor Party has become the party of those people who Burke singled out for his displeasure as leading France down the path to perdition after 1789, so has it has shed its Burkean skin for something much closer to Robespierre. The Liberal Party has not escaped unscathed from this process; it has had at least one leader who aspired to be a modern Napoleon. It has become a far more rationalist party.*

That the significance of Burke has changed for both political parties is a consequence of the reality, as Michael Oakeshott observed, that modern politics have become irreducibly rationalist in nature.[31] The older Australian tradition that focused largely on the tradition of responsible government and was built on an instinctive appreciation of practices derived from Australia's British inheritance has been seriously diluted.

Nevertheless, as James Allan has observed, Australia remains the last common law democracy in the Anglo world in which there is still significant opposition to any attempt to impose a bill of rights on the country.[32] This does not hide the reality that politics in Australia has been reframed in rationalist terms, which is to say that they have become much more explicitly ideological. Australians no longer see their political system as an inheritance that should be handed on in the best possible shape to succeeding generations. What this also means is that the tradition of natural utility, so well described by Norman, has been seriously jeopardised in its Australian setting.

One consequence of this change is that many of those who once would have claimed the Burkean mantle are moving much closer to Bolingbroke and a politics of nostalgia than to Burke and a politics of constructive reform. The Burkean legacy, including

---

* Following Oakeshott, by 'rationalist' I mean giving preference to models and abstract schemes as opposed to approaching a problem or issue in terms of the empirical facts involved. This mode of thought places greater emphasis on abstract ideas rather than skill based on experience.

the idea of natural utility, has been leached out of Australian political culture. After all, Bolingbroke, like Donald Trump, wished to make Britain great again by restoring the constitution corrupted by the Walpole Whigs.[33] Trump is indeed a 'patriot king'.[34]

This sort of mood is more subdued in Australia. There is a sense in liberal and conservative circles that 'all is not right' with the political world and that what is needed is a return to the good old days, represented by the prime ministership of either Sir Robert Menzies or John Howard, or perhaps an amalgamation of the two of them. There is a need for a 'patriot king' (or at least prime minister) to restore Australia and its way of life. Such a view rests on the notion that what passes for politics in the present is but a corruption of what was once great. Reform is not possible. In such a universe, how is it possible to be a Burkean conservative?

4

BURKE AND AUSTRALIAN LABOR

Michael Easson*

This essay suggests that Burkean ideas apply to the Australian labour tradition[1] and help illuminate that tradition as well as enabling the explication of competing ideas that sit outside, sometimes in competition and sometimes as complementary.

Part of the moral basis of commercial society, to allude to Jesse Norman's 2018 Glynn Lecture, is how various institutions, traditions, and people interact. What is the compass, the signpost, that guide them? What are, in Norman's words, "the basic questions of identity and legitimacy"? This leads me to consider Burke, in this case in the context of Australian Labor.

Now, it might be contended that Burke is a clear example of a conservative thinker. Former Liberal prime minister John Howard on various occasions proudly called himself a "Burkean conservative."[2] Norman and other writers have argued for Burke's credentials as the founder of modern conservative thinking.[3] There

---

* This essay is dedicated to John Murray Wheeldon (1929-2006), former ALP Senator and later Associate Editor and Editorial writer of *The Australian* newspaper, who first got me thinking about Burke and political theory. I would like to thank two friends, Dr Damian Grace and Catherine Harding, for comments on an earlier version of this essay.

is a vast literature to that effect, with some accounts more aware of Burke's makeover as a conservative than others.[4] How could anyone seriously suggest that, say, the idea of 'Burkean Labor' makes any sense?

Part of the argument is this: Burke is too subtle and provocative a writer to be entombed in a conservative's mausoleum, sealed off from contact with liberal and radical traditions with which he lived, contested, and debated.[5]

My thinking on the issues canvassed in this essay began thirty years ago, in question time after a lecture in Sydney, as someone extolled the so-called conservative credentials of Burke. A friend, John Wheeldon, suddenly turned round and snapped: "I thought he was a Whig, not a Tory!"

Burke was horrified that his own side of politics, the Whigs, might be captivated by the heady brew of 'liberty, fraternity, and equality' and he feared irresponsible intellectuals would seek bloody shortcuts to utopian solutions.[6] Without delving too deeply into this debate, there are several points to emphasise.

First, referencing Burke's defence of the Americans' right to self-government, the biographer and liberal political thinker, John Morley, in his neglected classic, *On Compromise*, wrote that "the French Revolution is alleged, and most unreasonably alleged, to have alienated him from liberalism."[7] But to the contrary, Morley sees Burke as the person to whom the Whigs and the liberal tradition "owed the whole vitality of their creed . . . that rational love of liberty, that antipathy to arbitrary ideas, on which rest their just claims to the gratitude of their descendants."[8] Burke is as interesting a liberal as he is a conservative.[9]

Second, this essay prefers to focus on these parts of the complex of Burke's writings:

1. Appreciation of the tension between liberty and tradition, including existing institutions and values;

2. Amelioration, rather than expropriation or extirpation, as the default reform approach;

3. An inclination to support more significant change where there is appreciation of the good that ought to be retained or amended;

4. Keenness to extend the sphere of liberty and independence of action.

All these principles are compatible with and, historically, are integral to the social democratic project.

There are admirers of Burke or certain ideas of Burke that are widely held by Labor thinkers and supporters. Over the years, some Labor MPs, for example, have emphasised support for Burke's view that a parliamentarian is elected to give judgement in the issues of the day, and is never a mere cipher for the imagined or even real views of an electorate.[10]

Those who saw the 2018 film, The Scribe,[11] on the life of Graham Freudenberg, speech writer to Labor Leaders from Calwell to Whitlam and Carr, might be surprised by a particular scene. The camera pans across Freudenberg's study picking up the portraits of Lincoln, Dr Johnson, Edmund Burke, and others. Freudenberg saw a soulmate in Burke's stirring rhetoric and intellectual arraignment of terror.

He is not alone. Early in the prime ministership of Bob Hawke, his then economic adviser, Dr Ross Garnaut, recalls: "When Graham Freudenberg and I discovered a shared appreciation of Burke during a Hawke visit to Mitterrand in 1983, we took advantage of a break in the official programme to visit Versailles and took turns in reading from *Reflections* on the steps of the Palace."[12]

In one important respect, sympathy for French ideals blinded many thinkers of the Left to reality. Emotionally, they would rather be on the opposite side to reaction. But this is a limiting and false dichotomy. Even if the choice were revolution versus defence of the existing order, such a juxtaposition is unreal and irrelevant to Australian politics today—where no one is arguing for anything madly revolutionary.

Barry Jones, even if his heart takes him in a different direction, acknowledges that Burke's analysis was prescient and brilliant. He writes: "The traditional/conservative view (set out with prophetic insight by Edmund Burke in October 1790) was to see man/woman in a received social context. . . People are born with a history, the product of organic processes. . ."[13] Jones is insightful to characterise Burke as a 'traditionalist' here. A conservative is committed to tradition. But it is also true that members of the labour movement, as discussed further in this essay, are committed to tradition—their own. A traditionalist approach can be a resource for a variety of political parties, such as Australian Labor.

In arguing about the relevance of Burke's ideas for the ALP it is necessary to mention, without overwhelming the reader, some of the issues in contention. And also to understand the political movement discussed.

Thus, this essay: First, touches on the Australian Labor Party from the perspective of the author who spent over forty years in the labour movement. Second, applies critical analysis and develops some working hypotheses about the Australian Labor tradition and Burkean ideals. Third, tests those hypotheses against several complications—including the party's Socialist Objective, and ideological rifts, and the context of economic reform under the Hawke/Keating government. Finally, rather than pinning Burke down as a Whig, radical, conservative, or liberal, it would be best to say his instinct, theory, and actions in favour of true liberty are an inspiration for the ages and, indeed, for the Australian labour movement.

Next I reflect on my experience of the ALP, politics through the lens of the local. All political parties have grassroots, where traditions grow and flourish, where the formation of new members begins, where the life of the party is renewed. At my first ALP branch, in Beverly Hills in suburban Sydney, most of the members and the leadership were mildly right-wing Labor, supportive of Whitlam, and interested in intra-party ideological conflict only at the margins.

I joined at the end of 1973 in my first year of university, applying after the November 1973 State election, the fourth loss in a row for NSW Labor against Premier Askin's Liberal/Country Coalition government; Whitlam was then in office as prime minister, elected on 2 December the previous year; Pat Hills was replaced as NSW Labor leader and as NSW leader of the opposition by Neville Wran.

My local branch's membership, all volunteers, included old timers, new migrants, and young people inspired by Whitlam and Wran.

Tom Togher, the branch president, a Commonwealth Bank manager, was a veteran of the ALP Group era when, several decades before, the Catholic Church in alliance with ALP moderates fought to wrest control off communist and communist-influenced sympathisers across the labour movement.[14]

In Young Street, Penshurst, where my family lived, ALP branch member Mike Klemencic, a public servant, resided across the road from my brother and me (we both joined around the same time). A Croatian migrant, he hated Tito, despised the far right-wing associations of some of his erstwhile compatriots ("Ustashi!") and deeply admired Whitlam. For him, Whitlam was like a refined European leader. I found Klemencic an inspiring figure, knowledgeable about contemporary global politics, an autodidact of the best sort—curious, provocative, and full of energy in discussing ideas, events, and personalities; radical in rhetoric, conservative in temperament.

His wife was starting university as a mature-age student and was critiquing the world through a feminist and mildly Marxist perspective. The latter annoyed her husband—and their spirited, though never terribly angry, debates were an education.

One of the Organisers of the Federated Rubber and Allied Workers' Union, George Le Fevre, was also a Beverly Hills branch member. He talked about the need to boost workers' compensation entitlements in his industry, characterised by unmasked work in fumy tyre factories, with manual labour prone to injuries, with lousy or non-existent redundancy or superannuation benefits. So many years later, I do not remember much of what he said. But I vividly recall his *fear* of stopping work through injury or retirement, and the prospect of living poorly.

Another new recruit was a final-year civil engineering student I remember only as Mr Booth, decidedly better dressed than anyone else, and also inspired by Whitlam. But he was regarded with suspicion in St George Young Labor, then in the hands of romantics aligned to the official ALP left (as they liked to see themselves), the NSW Unions and Labor Steering Committee.[15]

Looking back, the membership in this microcosm of the ALP in NSW were a sober, cautious lot, inspired by social democratic radicalism, conservative by inclination, optimistic about the potential for social change—in the main, idealists without illusions.

ALP branch meetings were routine boring affairs. The minutes of the last monthly meeting were read out loud; reports were given about party fora higher up—such as the State and Federal ALP electorate councils—to which the branch sent delegates. We met in a room a floor above the main bar in the Beverly Hills Hotel on King Georges Road. Some of the older members carried a schooner of beer into the meeting.

Vince Martin, the federal MP for the electorate of Banks, like Togher, a self-educated, decent Catholic Labor man, a former Australian Tax Office employee, would try to attend most meetings, Canberra Parliamentary sitting commitments permitting.

Kevin Ryan, narrowly unsuccessful in 1973 but victorious as Member for Hurstville in the 1976 State election, a result that with a couple of other wins became the difference that put Neville Wran QC into office as premier, visited the branch from 1974, as possible candidate, candidate, then MP.

Local representatives respected and consulted party members. As an ordinary party member, you learnt things that were not in the newspapers.

The social formation of budding activists was mostly outside of the formal meetings—the chats before and after, discussion while campaigning and in handing out leaflets, visiting other members' homes. There was camaraderie, a sense of a community that felt warmly tribal. Not that everyone agreed with each other.

Liberals were the other side, conservative and boring, the enemy, but not in a violent or any traducing sense. (The 'enmity index' increased after the Whitlam dismissal in November 1975. But the atmosphere in Australia was always a million miles from the turmoil of, say, Allende's Chile.)

Every new member wanted to learn about the battles of the past, hear answers to the question "Why did you join?" and thereby appreciate those elements that knitted us together in common cause.

As I moved around with family, out of home, and then in marriage, I found a similar spirit at Caringbah, Dulwich Hill, Croydon, and Enfield South in metropolitan Sydney.

In Caringbah branch in 1976 some of the legends of NSW Labor occupied the floor—or, rather, sat in the room at the local state school looking inconspicuous. There was Senator Arthur Gietzelt (ALP left faction leader) who was once part of the communist-aligned Hughes-Evans Labor Party in the 1940s; and Joe Riordan, pugnacious former national secretary and leader of the Federated Clerks Union, who in 1952 defeated Jack Hughes, the secretly communist national secretary of the union. Riordan was now an ex-Whitlam government minister. Defeated in 1975 as Member for Phillip in Sydney's eastern suburbs, Riordan tried to win back the seat in 1977 but lost again. A surprise was finding my former geography teacher at Sydney Technical High School in the branch. Reg Mawbey, ex-shearer, NSW secretary of the Australian Workers Union, was another Caringbah branch member. He drove to town early, sometimes spotting me walking down Port Hacking Road from Lilli Pilli, giving me a lift to town, puffing on his pipe, and in his slow drawl reminiscing on the country, union leaders, Hawke, Wran, what he thought were the things worth fighting for.

In his 1955 study on the ALP, Healey paid tribute to ". . . those unselfish, devoted little people . . . the 'wood and water joeys'. . . These are the people who tramp the streets with election literature, man the polling booths on election day, attend branch meetings . . . their hearts and minds are filled with all the great desires and visions for a better future, and as they lift leaders to the top, and all too frequently see them desert the cause, or fail to produce the things for which these people yearn, they try again with new representatives, for theirs is the soul that lives on hope and thrives upon disappointment."[16] Those words could have been written about the people I came to know. Perhaps the working class of those days has been 'forgotten'; the bonds of the labour movement need pertinent examples to be intelligible. Burke makes sense of those affinities in political terms. In Norman's words: "They are bound together by affection, identity and interest."

The more active you are, the more you think about the party. There is a deepening of commitment and understanding. Eventually, I extended involvement to attending the annual NSW State Conference in the glorious, cavernous Sydney Town Hall; becoming active in NSW Young Labor, linking up with a wider network across the country; engaging in local election campaigns; working for six months from the end of 1977 as a research officer for a new federal MP, the Member for Parramatta, ex-butcher turned abattoir owner and businessman, John Joseph Brown; then joining the Labor Council of NSW,[17] as education and research officer (succeeding Bob Carr); working for union leaders John Ducker, Barrie Unsworth, and John MacBean, and later, from 1989 to 1994, in their place as secretary of the Labor Council of NSW.

A number of features stand out.

First, the party, particularly the NSW ALP Right,[18] were conscientious moderates, interested in incremental change. The members were sincere, well-motivated souls who believed they were doing their bit to improve society by belonging to and participating, in small parts, in a movement. No one was messianic or a revolutionary radical. No one thought that theirs was a conservative inclination, certainly not overtly, but they did feel theirs was in keeping with the tradition, ethos and practice of the movement. The Labor historian Bede Nairn called the Labor reform impulse, "civilising capitalism", a laborious, dedicated effort to improve the world.[19] Undoubtedly, as I discuss below,

> Such a phrase raises many issues: including whether the civilising process is possible or desirable, what such an approach might mean in practice, what are the principles that might be called 'civilised', what capitalism is and whether 'civilising capitalism' is the beginning and end of the labour movement's objectives. Such issues are, of course, at the heart of the movement's history.[20]

Second, the party, again particularly the NSW ALP Right, were comfortable with strong leadership—that is, with values and ideas-driven leaders.[21] Whitlam and Wran exemplified that, as did Hawke and Keating after them. Perhaps there was the tinge of a religious aspect. ALP rhetoric frequently deploys phrases such as 'sacred duty' and the like.[22] Certainly, there is—or was—a strong sense of admiration for the leader, bordering on reverence for their saint-like calling.[23]

Third, it is characteristic that party members hold a deep respect and fascination for its history. Typically, members are conscious of reference points to past battles, the evolution of change, and disastrous mistakes. There was a fondness for thinking the ALP was the force for initiative and change, as against the other side being the party of inertia, with ALP party members joining out of a sense of purpose and curiosity of history. This also applied to the British Labour Party. Drucker, for example, writes: "The Labour Party has and needs a strong sense of its own past and of the past of the Labour movement which produced and sustains it. This sense of its past is so central to its ethos that it plays a crucial role in defining what the party is about to those in it."[24]

Fourthly, within the party there were different ideological currents, loosely left and right. Prior to the collapse of the Berlin Wall in November 1989, some elements on the ALP left were more or less sympathetic to Soviet communism and some others more statist (in the sense of thinking that government could solve everything) compared to the comfortable-with-the-mixed-economy ALP Right. Despite some wordy flourishes, no one advocated revolutionary change or the casting aside of the old for the new with blood-curdling rhetoric.

Interestingly, although some of the older members were scarred by the impact of the ALP split from 1955-1958, when ideological contest and division was intense, I never felt much of that, other than in foreign affairs debates (the Left in various shades of suspicion about the United States), and in knowing some of the individual histories.

A full appreciation of the party reveals that co-operation and radical liberal ideas stood in contrast to confrontation.[25] The party was a more eclectic and interesting phenomenon than that typically featured in party histories. Drucker suggests that too often academic accounts of the (British) Labour Party are written as if they were about the Fabian Society or the emergence of particular ideologies. But this is to miss the "ethos" and traditions, the rich layers of lore, that complement what might be particular policy nostrums and statements.[26] A similar point applies to Australia.

The restraint of Labor politics and its largely non-ideological character is Burkean. But just as important is the organic nature of ALP cohesion, apparent in its very formation, fed from various streams. My reminiscences of the party at the time I joined and subsequently show how Burkean attitudes permeated it. The association was organic and pluralist, but had immense respect for leaders and their 'hallowed' role. As Norman says of society, so too of a political party, "which links people together in an enormous and ever-shifting web of institutions, customs, traditions, habits, and expectations built up by innumerable interactions over many years."

What is the relevance of Burke to the labour movement experience that I have described? Looking at Burke's record is to note that he dealt with issues as they arose and applied his values and ideas to what he saw, reckoned with, and interpreted. To answer the question, "What did Burke stand for?" is to respond with reference to the issues and situations he contended with—the English revolution; American independence and the rights of colonial free settlers to govern themselves and, later, the need for conciliation with America; toleration for Ireland's Catholics; India and the limits of responsible overseeing and the protection of the rights of the people; and, most of all, the French Revolution, and its bloody parody of liberty, equality, and freedom, which consumed the last years of his life.

Burke comments in a speech on the American rebellion: "It is . . . a very great mistake to imagine that mankind follow up practically any speculative principle, either of government or of freedom, as far as it will go in argument and logical illation."[27] And soon after he says: "All government, indeed every human benefit and enjoyment, every virtue, and every prudent act, is founded on compromise and barter. We balance inconveniences; we give and take; —we remit some rights that we might enjoy others; and we choose rather to be happy citizens than subtle disputants."[28] Thus, it can be seen that Burke is suspicious of hard ideological or dogmatic positions being taken in the public square, oblivious to local or particular circumstances.

It might be useful to pause now and ask whether it is meaningful to speak of 'Burkean Labor'? Is it as strange a concept as, say, 'Ciceronian Labor' or 'Machiavellian Labor'? The terms demand explanation. One might find in Cicero's eloquence and fine values much inspiration. But the bloodlust, complacent racist superiority, and enslaving is unattractive. Machiavelli does not deserve his popular reputation as cynical ruthless adventurer, and there is a better case for extolling his name as relevant and insightful to the modern moment.[29] But even here, identification with a Renaissance figure requires much qualification and explication.

Is there a similar problem with the idea of 'Burkean Labor' and that name? Are the qualifications worthy of the term? Here is a justification: Respect for tradition need not be reactionary; in fact, it is compatible with labour ideals.[30] A politics focused on ameliorative policy rather than root-and-branch radicalism (still less revolution) are Burkean sentiments and inclinations. Harder to understand, to a modern mind, is Burke's opposition to a wide democratic franchise and his sentimentality towards the aristocratic filament of British society. Yes, Burke believed in property, hierarchy, and tradition, but he suggests pragmatic procedural paths to reform. Most significantly of all, as David Marquand puts it: "A profound, sometimes anguished fellow-feeling for the victims of arbitrary power ran, like a golden thread, through Burke's thirty years in parliament."[31] And this too, the cause of responsible liberty, is the golden thread of Australian Labor.

Without exhaustively mining modern Australian history for examples, one part of Burke's influence in Australia was through the role and impact of a distant nephew, Richard Bourke, Governor of New South Wales (1831-1837).[32] Bourke was a reformer who stood in opposition to religious prejudice, including from his own privileged Protestant social class; Bourke respected Catholics as fellow Christians.[33] He re-introduced trial by jury, championed the freedom of the press (despite their barbs), curtailed some of the worst features of arbitrary management of penal labour and recognised that prisoners too have rights. He championed transparency—including publishing the public accounts. A statue, erected in his honour in 1842, stands outside of the Mitchell Library in Sydney. In part the inscription reads:

> He voluntarily divested himself of the prodigious influence
> Arising from the assignment of penal labour, and enacted
> Just and salutary laws for the amelioration of penal discipline.
> He was the first governor who published satisfactory accounts
> Of the public receipts and expenditure,
> Without oppression or detriment to any interest,
> He raised the revenue to a vast amount and from its surplus,
> Realized extensive plans of immigration.
> He established religious equality on a just and firm basis,
> And sought to provide for all, without distinction of sect . . .

Bourke's approach to colonial government was a model for all subsequent administrations.[34]

Much later, from the 1870s onwards, the emergence of a labour movement in the colonies occurred as a result of a relatively liberal environment and in spite of determined and sometimes ferocious opposition. Many tributaries led to the formation of the Australian labour movement. Although its impulses were sometimes utopian, with dreamy romanticism mixed with hard-nosed industrial unionism, all this was forged into a political movement.

The cause never entirely won support from certain conservatives. The quest for legitimacy is an enduring theme in any history of the movement. Indeed, Freudenberg explicitly writes: "A sub-theme of this book [a history of NSW Labor] is Labor's never-ending struggle for legitimacy."[35] He goes on to say:

> For most of its history, the Labor Party has operated in a generally
> hostile environment. In the beginning, it faced the most obdurate
> combination of foes: the entire colonial establishment made up of
> the grazier, mine-owning, financial, professional and commercial
> interests of Sydney, philistine and provincial, but linked by mon-
> ey, marriage and memories, actual or borrowed, with the heart of
> the Empire in London.[36]

In Bede Nairn's account, by the end of the nineteenth century,
"it was clear that the Labor Party could only survive as a powerful
force if it adjusted its total activities to the requirements of the
electorate."[37] He went on to say, "working class radicalism did
not have to be abandoned, but it had either to shed formally its
extreme minority element or to contain it in an acceptable way."[38]
By the early twentieth century, Labor had taken root as a moderate
party, but not without tension in its identity. Manning Clark comments that "Labor wore many coats. It was the party of evolution
rather than revolution. It was also the party of paradoxes. . . Labor
had decided that to obtain political power in a capitalist society, it
must make a broad appeal."[39] Principles would have to bend.

This was sometimes seen as backsliding. Vere Gordon Childe
comments on the heterogeneity of the elements making up the
ALP, noting that "from its foundation the Labour Party has had to
look for allies outside of the working class."[40] Instead of seeing
this as strength, he complains, "Labour Governments have followed a vacillating policy and have tried to govern in the interests
of all classes instead of standing up boldly in defence of the one
class which put them in power."[41] Alas, Childe meant to explain
further his critique, but never completed the companion work he
hoped to write.[42]

Moderation and compromise is classic Burke. Although he
never used the word 'evolution'—Burke died before the term became popular—his approach to reform is always called evolutionary. The very fact that some Labor folk like Childe talk about

vacillation proves that Labor's moderate approach *is* Burkean—*pace* the conservatives. Labor objectives were still achieved but in a moderate way.

In Part 1 of *Reflections*, Burke says:

> opposed and conflicting interests . . . make deliberation a matter of necessity, not of choice; they make all change a subject of *compromise*, which naturally begets moderation; they produce *temperaments* that prevent the sore evil of harsh, crude, unqualified reformations, and rendering all the headlong exertions of arbitrary power, in the few or in the many, for ever impracticable. Through that diversity of members and interests, general liberty had as many securities as there were separate views in the various [parts of society] . . ."[43]

This is an argument for the governance of a society; the argument also applies to the creative development and application of policy in a political movement. In Norman's words: "It is in part the function of free institutions, as stores of memory and of politics, as channels for the articulation and reconciliation of conflicting views and interests, to be that national treasury of shared history and self-understanding." He refers to society; this also applies to a living political institution, to Australian Labor.

By the early twentieth century, reforms in Australia, won by backsliding or innovative compromise, in coalition within and without, stimulated by the labour movement in combination with other progressives, were seen as globally inspirational to liberals and social democrats, particularly in the United States. Reforms included the first minimum-wage laws, legislative support for conciliation and arbitration of industrial disputes, the secret ballot, female suffrage, mothers' pensions, and child welfare.[44]

Interestingly, significant elements of the intellectual left, seeing themselves as socialists aligned to mainstream Labor, were from the start in Australia opposed to Leninism and communist ideas. (This might be contrasted in the immediate years after the Bolshevik revolution with, say, Ireland, where significant parts of mainstream labour at least initially sided with revolutionaries, completely clueless as to what was going on—or what revolution meant.)[45]

Robert Samuel Ross, co-founder of the Victorian Socialist Party, mentor to future Labor prime minister, John Curtin,[46] and radical turned advocate of parliamentary and gradualist reform, wrote an influential pamphlet, *Revolution in Russia & Australia* (1920), which proposed an Australian alternative to the dictatorship of the proletariat. Ross was an advocate of union amalgams into industry unions, but he was critical of municipal and state-owned corporations, usually attached to Fabian ideas of socialism. He felt government by bureaucrats would be a new kind of tyranny. And he argued that the contrast between Russia and Australia was so vast that it would be a kind of madness to 'copy' Russian formulas. He proposed that radical objectives could be achieved through democratic means.[47]

Which now leads to a problem that has bedevilled the ALP in its long history: the issue of what it stands for. Much of the discussion centres on its Socialist Objective. This is to open a box the contents of which have a complicated pedigree and interpretation, covered extensively elsewhere. Frequently overlooked, however, are the guild socialist and Catholic principles that informed the choice of words that originally defined the term.[48] In an essay on the Objective, Gareth Evans refers to the "familiar socialist language" in the wording of the 1921 Objective and "in particular the expression 'socialisation of industry, production, distribution and exchange'."[49] In saying so, Evans missed a key element. The term 'socialisation' instead of 'nationalisation' suggests that something other than merely expropriating capital was in mind.[50]

Indeed, that is so. The idea was that 'socialising' meant the organisation of industry on democratic lines, a form of self-government in industry.

Professor Meredith Atkinson, from personal correspondence,

quotes Bob Ross explaining the socialisation objective: "The new objective was consciously designed as a process in social reconstruction, and I feel that all earnestly seeking the New World of peace and plenty should be trumpeting its sincerity and efficiency."[51]

Atkinson drily comments that "Mr Ross is a whole-souled idealist, who has lived his whole life in the movement, and it is perhaps to his credit that he can find 'greatness and genius in the co-ordination shown in the linking-up as a synthesis the theories of Constitutional Labourism, Guild Socialism, Syndicalism and Social Democracy'."[52]

Ross protested that, in the heady atmosphere of the time, "Would you have had the Trades Union Congress commit itself to bloody revolution? Its greatness, I think, was in holding finely and firmly to the view that Australian development, character, common sense and attainments along the lines of democracy warranted further trust in these proved lines of action."[53] He went on to proffer: "Guild Socialism, I beg to say, in nothing of its philosophy or principles even faintly suggests the holocaust of blood which the critic . . . sees as inherent in it."[54]

But these ideas—socialisation, worker control and the like—could be criticised as meaning different things. At the Brisbane Conference of the ALP in 1921, the Socialist Objective resolution was opposed by the entirety of the New South Wales delegation and Maurice Blackburn, a Victorian delegate. Before the Conference ended, Blackburn moved a resolution calling on the Conference to 'interpret' the resolution to mean socialisation to the extent required to eliminate exploitation. This wording crept into the official ALP Platform in the mid-1940s.[55]

As statist and communist influences grew stronger in the Australian labour movement (and the movement developed amnesia about its own history), the distinction between socialisation and nationalisation faded to such an extent that the Blackburn Declaration became an escape card for allegations that the movement was communist in doctrine and aim. This particularly appealed to certain right-wing Labor types. For example, Frank McManus mentions in his memoirs that he wrote for *Freedom* during World War II in defence of Labor's Socialist Objective, but in sympathy with the Blackburn Declaration.[56] Chifley, on the defensive in the 1949 election campaign, insisted: "It is not the objective of the Labor Party to go around socialising everything, but to do things for the good of the people."[57]

Race Mathews's book, *Of Labour and Liberty: Distribution in Victoria 1891-1966*, on the Victorian labour movement and the impact of Catholic social thinking is useful in recovering some of the traditions lost as a result of the Labor splits in the 1950s.[58] To this analysis might be added Lloyd Ross's articles published for the Catholic intellectual journal, *Twentieth Century*, in the late 1940s and early 1950s.[59]

The Objective, following a long preamble, now reads: "The Australian Labor Party is a democratic socialist party and has the objective of the democratic socialisation of industry, production, distribution and exchange, to the extent necessary to eliminate exploitation and other anti-social features in these fields." The qualifier, "to the extent necessary", is the essence of Blackburn.

Arguably two of the greatest of Labor achievements are the introduction of universal health insurance (Medicare)[60] and a national system of compulsory superannuation—both achieved during the Hawke-Keating years. Interestingly, in explaining and defending the latter, Burke's name was invoked.[61] Before those reforms were attempted, at the beginning of the Hawke government, the deregulation of the financial markets was pursued.

After it won office in 1983, Labor floated the Australian dollar, removed some of the restrictions in competition affecting the banking sector, licensed foreign banks to enter the market, and cajoled the sector to lend more and be more entrepreneurial in supporting Australian businesses. The full impact of those reforms is still playing out.

The changes raised the question of whether Labor was turning its back on long-cherished Labor principles. This was played out at various fora across the party, for example at the NSW ALP Conference in June 1984 held at the Sydney Town Hall. The ALP Left honed onto the argument that Hawke and Keating were moving away from Labor traditions. Ben Chifley, who tried to nationalise the banks in 1949, would be turning in his grave, they said.

Keating went to the microphone on the floor of Conference, surrounded by battalions of right-wing unions, usually joyful at the gladiatorial fights of Left and Right, but momentarily stilled by doubt. Dressed in a black Zegna suit, white shirt, red tie, Keating thundered that the banks in Australia were run by dull executives from Sydney's North Shore, and were incurious about helping a new business, or expanding an existing one; they lazily acted within the confines of a cosy oligopoly, unhurried by the market or the task of feeding capital to creative employers of labour.

In one stroke, he turned the debate around, saying something like, "I'll tell you who the real conservatives are. They are in the metal workers' union. Ben Chifley would be turning in his grave if he heard the nonsense spouted at this conference. With the so-called Left defending those members of the Turramurra branch of the Liberal party instead of championing good Labor Party reform."[62]

Keating's hands waved, cutting the air. At times his arms lunged over both sides of the microphone like Count Dracula in full flight, preparing to attack. He forced the audience, his audience of suburban branch members, bush and regional representatives, and unionists, to think harder instead of merely acting and reacting to the slogans uttered so far. He referenced history. Instead of repudiating the labour heritage, Keating embraced it, wrapped himself in Chifley iconography and argued that a modern ALP had to govern for the times. Each era is different but nothing happens in a vacuum or, on his watch, without regard to party and tradition.

Arguably, this was the high-water mark of leaders and rank-and-file engaging in full-throttle debate about what should be done, when, how, and by whom. Keating later wrote of his approach: "Free of the shackles of any rigid ideology and remaining alive to the lessons of a changing world there should be little that Labor cannot achieve in its quest to fulfil its original and essential charter—to improve the lot of the common people."[63] Thus, rhetoric and practice were conjoined. This reflects a Burkean view of positive change in the context of tradition and contemporary challenges.

In conclusion, 'Burkean Labor' may never be a banner unfurled over the balustrades at an ALP conference at the Sydney Town Hall. The association of 'Burke' with 'conservative' may be too strong. Burke has been appropriated by conservatives. But they do not own him, for the reasons stated herein.

In puzzling over the complexity of modern politics, in seeking the light of insight from the past, Norman invokes Burke, his "great political hero". Burke belongs not just to one side of politics. My response is to argue that the organic nature of the ALP is a particularly sound pragmatic argument against complete conservative appropriation. This makes the argument about the relevance of Burke to Labor. The truth is that affinities in labour—and Labor—are much closer to Burke's ideals than the narrow individualism that permeates modern conservative parties.

From the discussion in this essay, it is clear that to see Burke as a figure foreign to the achievement of sensible reform is an occluded perspective. Certainly, the Australian labour tradition embraces a keen appreciation of the practical limitations of existing society, the importance wherever possible of improving, rather than overthrowing, without being shy about ambitiously seeking to extend reform in more radical ways, should that extend liberty's sphere and encourage greater freedom of a non-servile people. Norman references Burke in saying of the social order: "It is an inheritance, which imposes on each generation the obligation to preserve and if possible to enhance it, before passing it on to the next generation." Australian Labor, with its constant invocation of its heritage, its members' sense of history and purpose, is Burkean.

This essay could do no more than outline a positive argument about the relevance of Burkean ideas to unrevolutionary Australian Labor. Even when utopian ideas threatened to engulf the party, ideas of civilising capitalism (a viewpoint seeking to preserve what is best in the system while civilising the rest) prevailed. The many ways this politics of Burkean moderation has played out in the Labor Party deserves the further investigation of other researchers who may develop, contest, enrich, and elaborate on them.

5

Markets, morals and Australian Labor governments

Amanda Walsh

Jesse Norman is right: market fundamentalism is dead. No one believes any longer—if they ever did—that economics is a clean scientific enterprise devoid of morals, values, and other markers of humanity.

In his lecture, Norman argues that morals are, in fact, inherent in commercial society: the very fact of human interaction, expressed in innumerable mundane ways, creates and reinforces the "mutual obligations and personal regard" that provide commercial life with its moral compass.

Extending Norman's argument slightly, this framework of morals and values reaches beyond the marketplace, and is heavily in evidence in the halls of power. In the sphere of democratic government, economic policy has always been subject to a contest of ideas and values, as elected representatives determine priorities (and privilege) in the allocation of resources. Over the last few decades, the contest of ideas in economic policy has often seemed a shadow play: the triumph of neoliberalism has largely homogenised the political economy, such that disagreement between political parties over economic policy occurs mostly at the margins. However, even mainstream political parties manage to express their views of humanity and morality through their economic policies.

This response to Norman's essay addresses his view that the left has failed to address the big issues in political economy, and asks whether it holds true in the Australian context. Norman's lecture is explicitly British in its scope: not only through his emphasis on Burke and Smith, but in his application of their theses to modern British society and politics. With some scorn, Norman accuses the left of British politics of failing to engage seriously, or competently, with issues in modern political economy.* While much of Norman's argument is accessible and acceptable to an Australian audience, not all of it rings true. In particular, his dismissal of the British left sits uneasily with the Australian experience in the era of neoliberalism. This response therefore provides the context in which to judge the role of the Australian left, and to demonstrate its singular role in riding, and directing, the wave of neoliberalism that hit Australia in the 1980s.

For Norman, the British left failed in two key moments of the modern political economy: first, in the wake of the collapse of the Soviet empire in 1989-91; and second, following the global financial crisis of 2007-08. Let us focus first (if briefly) on the latter period, when governments of the left were in place in both the United Kingdom and Australia.

Experiences of the global financial crisis were very different in the United Kingdom and Australia. The British prime minister,

---

* While Norman does not offer a definition of 'the left', his reference to Tony Blair and Gordon Brown suggests that he means, principally, the British Labour Party. I would ordinarily use the term 'centre-left' to denote both the British Labour Party and the Australian Labor Party, but I will stick with Norman's 'left' in responding to his essay.

Gordon Brown, presided over "a massive increase in borrowing" in order to shore up financial institutions, which saw government borrowing balloon from 2.3 percent of GDP in 2007–08 to 11.3 percent in 2008–09. Despite the increase in government debt, the British economy fell into recession and unemployment jumped immediately.[1]

Conversely, Australia is widely regarded as having had a 'good' global financial crisis. The incoming Labor government of Kevin Rudd acted swiftly to stimulate household spending, economic activity, and jobs (particularly in construction), channelling more than $50 billion into the economy.[2] Australia also enjoyed relatively low exposure to the imploding American housing market and banking sector, combined with stringent lending standards for Australian banks. At the same time, demand in China for Australian resources was booming.[3] On the back of these interventions (and structural advantages created during the Hawke-Keating governments), Australia was one of only two advanced economies to avoid recession during the crisis.

The mass unemployment and lingering economic lethargy experienced in much of the developed world was avoided in Australia. The Rudd government's willingness to deploy sharp economic tools to shore up household finances and employment was entirely in keeping with labour views about the role of the state in economic policy. However, to understand fully the differences between the governing left in the United Kingdom and in Australia, we need to focus on an earlier period—the 1980s, which was pivotal for the relationship between morals and the market, and the mediating role of the state.

The rise of neoliberalism has changed utterly the relationship between the state and the market. Arriving on the political stage in the late 1970s and early 1980s, neoliberalism was a reaction (or an overreaction) to the stagflation gripping western economies at that time. Neoliberalism, in its most pure form, ought to mark the triumph of a certain view of human value and how it should be measured—by the market, at arm's length from the state. In fact, in order to guarantee individual freedom, the state needed only to provide private property rights, the rule of law, and free markets. The ensuing private enterprise and innovation would generate wealth, which would trickle down through the economy. Proponents of neoliberalism were "deeply opposed" to state intervention in the market.[4] Thus, the scientific, clean lines of the market would replace the values-based, socio-economic engineering of Keynesianism.

At the vanguard of neoliberal policymaking stood the British prime minister, Margaret Thatcher, and President Ronald Regan in the United States. They both headed ostensibly conservative governments, but their economic policies were distinctly radical, excising the state from its customary mediating role between citizens and capital.

In contrast, Australia began its relationship with neoliberalism (as the dominant ideology of the state) under a Labor government, which sought to ameliorate the most negative effects of what Australians came to know as 'economic rationalism' through policies to protect wages and enhance provision of social services, such as health and education. The radical economic agenda of the prime minister, Bob Hawke, and the treasurer, Paul Keating, sat alongside a 'traditional' Labor concern for jobs, wellbeing, and social cohesion.

The epitome of these intersecting goals may be the Accord.* Countless words (many of them contested) have been expended on the political and economic effects of the Accord on Australia and the labour movement. Suffice it to say, the Accord was managed by the Hawke government in such a way that it protected the image of old-style union-led policymaking, while embedding

---

* To give the document its full title, "Statement of Accord by the Australian Labor Party and the Australian Council of Trade Unions regarding Economic Policy".

neoliberalism in the heart of Australia's economic structures.

The Accord was centred on the goal of full employment, and planned to use price controls, centralised wage fixation, taxation reform, and wide-ranging social reforms to strike a balance between the interests of trade unions and capital. Once in government, however, Hawke ensured that the agreement underwent "selective application, modification and renegotiation".[5] In fact, the economic and social effects of the Accord "were perhaps not as important as its symbolism, and the uses to which this could be put".[6] Brandishing the Accord, the Hawke government was able to launch sweeping economic reforms, including the reduction of industry protection measures such as tariffs, while still pushing its credentials as the workers' party.

This pairing of neoliberal economic policy with a social justice platform was emblematic of the Hawke and Keating governments, and remains a touchstone of modern Labor in Australia.

Within the Labor Party, the relationship between neoliberal economics and social democratic principles requires ongoing attention and enunciation. It is no surprise that an 'inequality agenda' sits at the heart of the Labor project in Australia, attempting to bridge the divide between capitalist expansion and individual wellbeing. For Labor, the challenge is to maximise market-based economic growth while ensuring that no-one is left behind. In the words of the Labor National Platform, "excessive inequality detracts from economic growth and damages the social fabric".[7]

The Labor project to minimise inequality has explicitly community-based (or communitarian) goals. If society is not stratified, if no one is left behind, how much easier will it be to pool our resources of wit and will to advance both the economy and the community? In fact, the contemporary Labor view of society recalls Jesse Norman's observations on the need to "preserve and enhance the social order in the public interest", for which he cites Burke.

Where does this leave us? Perhaps the best way to measure the triumph of the market is to consider the distance travelled since the global financial crisis of 2007-08. During the crisis, the anti-neoliberal bandwagon groaned under the weight of political leaders seeking to reassert the role of the state in the economy—and evoking Richard Nixon's famous observation (from another era of financial strife) that "we are all Keynesians now".

More than a decade later, it is clear that the global financial crisis merely disrupted the status quo of neoliberal policymaking, and equilibrium in the political economy returned remarkably quickly. What appeared, in very embryonic form, to be a triumph of the left quickly dissipated.[8] Was the global economic crisis a missed opportunity? Not at all—in fact, parties of the left reacted precisely as we might have expected, given their embrace of neoliberalism in the early 1980s. There is no going back to Keynesianism.

However, neither are parties of the left attracted to pushing the boat out still further. Whether through a heartfelt connection to its traditions, or a more cynical attempt to harness voter anger at market failings, the ALP appears unlikely to wade deeper into the darker waters of market-led economics. Of course, only time will tell, and perhaps Labor's shock loss in the 2019 federal election will force a reconsideration of just how much value voters place on the traditional Labor platform of education, health, and social support, on a base of (light-touch) wealth redistribution.

In the final analysis, these are all questions of degree. Market fundamentalism has always been curtailed by political reality, ideology, and pragmatism. There is no such thing as 'pure' neoliberalism in practice, and so morals will always influence the market—not only at the level of individual human interactions, but also at the level of state policy. Where the balance lies—between individual success and the common good—will always be contested in Australia, but within an arena that now accepts market-based solutions to problems across the social spectrum.

6

THE LIMITS OF
NATURAL UTILITY

LEANNE SMITH

Dr Jesse Norman's lecture is indeed timely in the context of to-day's confused and fraught world. I congratulate him for his pro-motion of respectful debate and cross-political engagement, both in this lecture and through his political and academic work more broadly. As he himself says, "Politics today is dying for lack of friendliness, warmth and decency. Everyone deserves to be heard, calmly, respectfully and with moderation." I trust Dr Norman will accept this response to his lecture in that spirit.

In describing the 'moral panic' around the nature of modern society, Norman very skilfully articulates some age-old funda-mental questions that have concerned philosophers from the East and West not just for the last four hundred years, but since the times of Plato and Confucius. Norman asks,

> What is the nature of modern society? What sustains it? Why should we give it our continued loyalty as citizens, as individuals, as human beings? Why should we help others outside our imme-diate families and friends? Why should we make any sacrifices for others, come to that, if we have nothing in common with them? And who is this *we*, anyway?

Norman is right to describe the challenges facing our modern individual societies and our shared world in this profound way.

However, whether his defence of what he describes as the moral basis of a commercial society, 'natural utility', provides helpful answers to these very real and urgent questions, I would challenge.

Norman acknowledges what he describes as "a kind of moral panic about the nature of modern society" in contemporary debate. He identifies a range of social ills prevalent in "modern society", from drug abuse to single motherhood; falling social mobility to economic division; distrust in authority to unaccountable leadership; culture wars to loss of identity.

While he also acknowledges that much of the blame for these problems is today focused on free trade and capitalism, he does not say whether he agrees with such a diagnosis, nor does he offer his own. Instead he offers 'commercial society' as the antidote—but to what? Furthermore, he fails to make a convincing distinction between free-market capitalism and the commercial society he advocates for. He also makes no reference to the mounting critiques of neoliberalism, as distinct from classical liberalism. These ambiguities, whether intended or not, undermine the philosophical rigour of Norman's argument.

Norman briefly documents what he describes as the move away from all-embracing acceptance of capitalism, starting with the financial crisis of 2007-2008 and the rise of the Occupy Wall Street Movement, the intensified polarisation of politics (between urban/rural, young/old, or the so-called somewhere/anywhere voters), and the populist appeals that feed on those divisions and fears. He attributes policy failures to both sides of politics in terms of regaining the centre ground and notes that "tribes started to form that talked more and more not to others, but to themselves."

It is from this trajectory that Norman appears to arrive at the issue on which his defence of the moral basis of a commercial society seems to stand—that this reaction away from free-market capitalism, combined with polarisation and populism, is leading to "extreme schemes of nationalisation, expropriation, and state control". It is this element of the lecture I would have liked Norman to explicate more thoroughly, both in the British context and internationally. Is a return to extreme forms of state intervention what Norman is warning against, by making his case for the moral basis of a commercial society?

Norman begins by dismissing, quite summarily, four weighty philosophical traditions—the natural law of philosophers like John Locke for its outdated notions; social contract theory of the likes of Thomas Hobbes for the circularity of its logic; the categorical imperative theory of Immanuel Kant for being unrealistic; and finally the utilitarianism of Jeremy Bentham and John Stuart Mill for being context blind. There are of course other traditions, and other philosophers, who have much to say on the questions Norman posited above, to which I will refer throughout this response.

Based on his own extensive academic research of two towering historical figures—political theorist Edmund Burke and economist Adam Smith—Norman then merges his preferred approach, that of 'natural utility'. But first, he considers Burke and Smith's influence separately, and so shall I.

Beginning with Burke, Norman's theory accepts as a starting point the existing social order prevailing in any given society:

> Each has a social order, which links people together in an enormous and ever-shifting web of institutions, customs, traditions, habits and expectations built by innumerable interactions over many years.

To illustrate this point, he turns to eighteenth-century England. If the purpose of the lecture is to demonstrate how this acceptance of the social order helps us grapple with the challenges of today, a more contemporary example might have strengthened his argument.

More of an issue for me, though, is that Burke and Norman's

reliance on the inherent goodness of the social order is blind to the biases, injustices, inequities, and abuses built into all social orders. Norman does not acknowledge the power imbalances that, by human nature, dominate within these social orders. As British philosopher Harriet Taylor Mill said, "Power makes itself the centre of moral obligation".[1] Norman makes no acknowledgement that the very institutions he cites as balancing state power in reality work very differently for people, or not at all, depending on where one fits in that social order. His is indeed a very privileged perspective from someone at the elite end of the social order.

To share just a handful of examples, at least in the Australian context, let us consider how the legal system serves women who are victims of domestic violence, or how detention and correction facilities serve Aboriginal people; how churches and other institutions of trust have permitted the abuse of children under their care; how people with disabilities are able to access education and work opportunities; how government and business are undermining the rights and working conditions of workers, for example through the elimination of penalty rates.

To the people I speak of here, Norman's assertion that these institutions of the social order "give shape and meaning to people's lives, at work or play, setting rhythms to the day or year, creating overlapping identities and personal loyalties" is quite simply adding insult to injury.

Norman admires the social order, as Burke portrays it, from the outside—not examining how power dynamics and access to opportunity affect an individual's place within that order. An individual's view of the social order will certainly be shaped by the respect and worth they are afforded within it. This is true for all societies, including those that *may* be more peaceable, effective, and successful than others. Norman's take on the merits of the social order almost represent his own version of utilitarianism— as long as the social order 'works' writ large, its impact on some individuals is irrelevant. He might as well come out and say, "The ends justify the means."

According to Burke's description, "the social order is . . . sublime. It is an inheritance, which imposes on each generation the obligation to preserve and if possible, enhance it, before passing it on to the next generation". If this legacy is what forms the moral basis of a commercial society, then clearly that moral basis tolerates inherent inequality, for a social order is just that—an order—and a person can be at the top or the bottom of it. Norman accepts the condition that what is to be preserved does not benefit all in society relatively (or even remotely) equally. It may be a logical goal for the notorious one percent, but what incentive do those at the bottom have to preserve such a social order for themselves or their children?

I shall return to Norman's idea of an 'intergenerational partnership' when considering the morals of commercial society as applied to environmental protection.

In his treatment of Adam Smith, Norman quite rightly points to the much richer range of intellectual contributions Smith made beyond market economics and capitalism. When Smith wrote about commercial society at the time of the Industrial Revolution, he spoke of "a process which had unleashed huge prosperity, spreading wealth and replacing personal subordination with economic relationships of interdependence". Smith saw this economic interdependence as creating mutual obligations, and one can understand the reason for his optimism at this point in history. However, the idea that market exchange breeds an empathy in people is an issue of contention.[2] But one wonders how Norman sees this economic interdependence playing out in today's global economy, dominated by powerful multinational corporations that routinely slip the reigns of accountability for the harms they cause to people and the planet.

Norman's assessment of Smith's belief that these mutual obligations would not only be economic but social and that moral values are not internal but come from human interaction is that "This mutual interaction and empathy . . . becomes the basis for moral norms . . . takes on a public life of its own and becomes authoritative".

Norman does explain how, in his view, mutual economic obligation could lead to mutual social obligation, through the elements of a society that build up around an economy. However, these elements emerge in all societies, regardless of their economic systems. It is far-fetched to attribute them to any one economic system. What his lecture lacks is a deeper explanation of Smith's and his own assumption that economic mutual obligation necessarily leads to sympathy and, further, to empathy. How does the transactional evolve into the emotional—especially today?

It seems the link between economic engagement and empathy would require a clearer definition of who is the 'we' in Norman's earlier set of fundamental questions. This goes to whom we count within our tribe and how we perceive and treat the 'other' within or connected to these social orders.

Let's consider for a moment, in this context, the policy and practice of slavery and the slave trade in the United Kingdom and across its colonies, which of course historically extended before and after the time of both Burke and Smith. Whether we speak of the workhouse, or convict transportation, or trading in human beings as slaves, there surely is a problem for Norman in his assertion that commercial society breeds empathy. In this light, his claim is absurd.

Norman then brings Burke and Smith together and asserts that "the moral basis of commercial society lies in the ceaseless exchange of mutual obligations and personal regard." He says its values are hard work, enterprise, creativity, and thrift.

And yet, Martin Luther King Jr reminds us, while dealing with the intergenerational legacy of one aspect of Burke's social order:

We have deluded ourselves into believing the myth that Capitalism grew and prospered out of the protestant ethic of hard work and sacrifice. The fact is that Capitalism was built on the exploitation and suffering of black slaves and continues to thrive on the exploitation of the poor both black and white, both here and abroad.[3]

Earlier in his lecture, Norman acknowledges that this tradition of natural utility has escaped academic notice—and we may well at this point ask, "Why?" And further, how does Norman usefully apply this tradition to the contemporary challenges he identifies at the outset of his lecture?

Norman does make a slight admission of the limitations of this theory: "There will be societies in which the boot-strapping process by which freedom created freedom cannot take place, because not enough of its people have boots on their feet at all". One can only assume Norman is talking about social orders in some of those less successful countries, not countries like the United Kingdom or Australia. Which is a shame, given the growing disparities of income, wealth, and opportunity within our two countries. This bootstrap analogy may be the most out-of-touch and unfortunate statement in this lecture. It reflects the perspective of the top end of the 'sublime' social order—wealthy, white, privileged, able, and male—condescending to the rest of us with the fabulous notion that any and all opportunity is there to seize, if only we choose to do so (statistics on social mobility be damned).[4]

Norman would do well to consider how the Golden Rule, expressed in numerous world religions, would assess the merits of the social order he advocates. Or perhaps to reconsider Rawls's 'original position', where in designing a social structure we are all behind a veil of ignorance, knowing nothing of ourselves, our natural abilities, or our position in society. Would he then have so much faith in the social order?

In further defence of the commercial society, Norman speaks of other countries that have succumbed to fascism and communism as fatally displacing the human need for meaning. Does he think commercial society is immune to this loss? Is he aware of the suicide rates in our developed market economies? Should he look to his own country today, where around 320,000 homeless people do not have the luxury of searching for meaning, but must direct all their energies to daily survival?[5]

Norman's assessment of the morals and history of commercial society is obviously rooted in his own experience of life within the United Kingdom—his focus is the Anglosphere. I would only suggest that if one is going to take one's show on the road, one should be aware of the broader intellectual and experiential context.

His potted history of the evolution of society leaves out significant tracts. Norman provides two models to compare—commercial society (good) and fascism/communism (bad). He leaves out anything in between. I shall briefly note just two relevant developments here.

First, consideration of the practice of social democracy. Social democracy is a political, social, and economic ideology that supports economic and social interventions to promote social justice within the framework of a capitalist economy. Perhaps best illustrated in post-war Europe, which pivoted from war to shared prosperity in little more than a generation,[6] it has also been a significant feature of Australian political history.[7]

Secondly, Norman completely ignores the enormous impact on our two societies and many others of the development of international human rights law—to which of course the United Kingdom and Australia are both bound—and the civil rights movements. (Human rights monitoring under the 1975 Helsinki Accords was a critical point of leverage in the eventual downfall of the Soviet Union, an event Norman presumably views as a victory for his 'commercial society'.)

When Norman says, "That idea—that things might be possible in Australia that would not be possible anywhere else in the world", it might well apply to Australia's own unique experience with and development of social democracy. In terms of its philosophical underpinnings, I would draw on the work of John Dewey:

> The conception of the common good, of general well-being, is a criterion which demands the full development of individuals in their distinctive individuality . . . only when individuals have initiative, independence of judgement, flexibility, fullness of experience, can they act so as to enrich the lives of others and only in this way can a truly common welfare be built up. The other side of this statement, and of the moral criterion, is that individuals are free to develop, to contribute and to share, only as social conditions break down walls of privilege and of monopolistic possession.[8]

In the 1970s and 1980s, first under prime ministers E. G. Whitlam and then R. J. L. Hawke, Australia was moving in a vastly different direction from the neoliberal path of privatisation and deregulation that would evolve in the United Kingdom under Thatcher and the United States under Reagan. Australia was building a nation for all its citizens, focused on a strong economy but also with a strong focus on social justice; with a social safety net that protected and uplifted the weak as well as the strong. Universal healthcare, free tertiary education, equal pay for women, support for single mothers, and the extension of services to those on the margins of our cities and regional areas, as well as protections against discrimination, were just some of the policies developed during this period to strengthen the social compact and empower future generations. Although under attack today, this proud legacy of social democracy is still in our bones, and its continued relevance is tragically apparent in the vast inequities our societies face today.

To fail to recall the lessons of the human degradations experienced in the First and Second World Wars and the emergence of the post-war consensus—including the Universal Declaration of

Human Rights—is a serious gap in Norman's analysis of how we relate to each other as citizens and members of society. The development of international human rights law and the way nations across the world have sought collectively to balance the dignity and needs of all individuals with the needs of societies has done much in both our countries to level inequalities and strengthen communities. Under human rights law, the moral basis of a flourishing society is the acceptance and defence of the equal dignity and respect deserved by and afforded to every person. Like it or not, this recognition forms a fundamental part of the legacy we have inherited, and cannot be ignored.

Norman argues that markets and morals cannot be separated because both depend on the human capacity for empathy and exchange. I refer to my earlier comments about the state of inequality, indifference, and polarisation within our respective societies and markets, and in those globally, to challenge this assertion. He contends that markets rely on human acquiescence or consent—this is what we all signed up for—but he reveals no awareness of the power imbalances that force individuals to make terrible choices for the sake of survival, such as what might make a desperate mother in one country offer her child to a sexual predator. Or why a casual worker in another would take a Sunday shift now, even though she has lost her penalty rates, because being able to pay the rent is more important than standing up for her rights.

Returning to what Norman says about the intergenerational partnership, that this 'natural utility' model is not designed to satisfy the needs of any individual or generation, but to preserve the social order in the public interest—how would he apply this claim to our commercial market-based societies' management of our natural environment? Surely this is the most important legacy we hold for future generations and the public interest.

Stephen Gardiner's 2011 essay, "A Perfect Moral Storm: Climate Change, Intergenerational Ethics and the Problem of Moral

Corruption", outlines the complex political and policy challenges, vested interests, and power dynamics that paralyse our ability to perceive the threat accurately and to make the best decisions for our common future. The most affluent today live at the expense of the poor, the next generations, and the natural world itself. This is moral corruption, wherein present-day individuals and societies alike knowingly hold all the power over their future counterparts, and yet are drawn to compromise the greater good (i.e., the future) for the material demands of the here and now.

The final point Norman makes is about capital and social capital. He argues we have good historical capital in our societies, and we should not shun it in "fits of contemporary rage". My response is that the value of the legacy of that capital depends on where you sit in the social order, and that the failure of our social order and commercial society to ensure that capital is shared, and that every human being is afforded the same dignity is what has led us here. Norman's construction of the 'we'—the dead, the living, and the unborn—still leaves out so much of today's humanity. And that's why it can't be a solution to the challenges we face within our communities and across the globe.

Dr Norman's lecture raises more questions than it purports to answer. In the end, the model of natural utility he describes, based on the moral basis of a commercial society, fails to provide answers to any of the challenges he posits.

7

CONSTRAINTS TO
MARKET EXCHANGE

CRIS ABBU

Jesse Norman provides a thoughtful articulation of the moral basis of a commercial society. He draws on the works of Edmund Burke and Adam Smith and argues that the moral nature of society is based on a market mechanism. This process of commercialisation of society creates wealth and value, and results in cooperative relationships that are both economic and moral. Of great significance, as acknowledged by Norman, is that these exchanges create ethical and social norms and with these norms come moral practices and moral institutions.

Norman is not the first to extol the value and virtues of a commercial society where unencumbered markets operate.[1] A commercial society is noble because it creates value and is predicated on freedom. It is based on free agents acting on their mutual interests. No one is coerced to exchange. It is this characteristic of free individuals engaging in "ceaseless exchange" that makes it also efficient and effective. On the other hand, the virtue of a commercial society is diminished and rendered inadequate if it does have the corresponding economic virtue as in the case of thin markets exemplified by the National Disability Insurance Scheme (NDIS).

Economics tells us that, in any market exchange, individuals aim to maximise their utility. Implicit in this utility-maximising goal is the notion of competition. Competition in its simplest terms is the presence of choices, of alternatives. As individuals are assumed to be rational, given a set of competing alternatives, individuals choose the best outcomes (the greatest value possible) for themselves, subject to their own personal constraints. Hence, when an exchange or transaction happens and is realised, the individuals involved in the transaction are deemed to be in a 'happy' state because the transaction is profitable to them, and their goal of maximising utility is achieved.

In economics parlance, this is the equilibrium point where both seller and buyer agree to the exchange and attain outcomes that are mutually beneficial and mutually reinforcing. This is the situation that is desired by everyone. This exchange is efficient and effective because the greatest value is extracted by the parties in the exchange—voluntarily at that. Hence, Norman is on point in saying that markets are good because, like any human institution, they rely on mutual benefits and human acquiescence. And it is this acquiescence or choice that is so integral to markets that can also spell their own demise. I am referring to the demise of markets that occurs in the absence of choice.

Jesse Norman warns of institutions that usurp the freedoms of a commercialised society and of societies where freedom cannot take place. What Norman fails to mention is that there are markets where freedoms are inherently curtailed. In other words, there are certain market structures that can limit or obliterate individual choice. I make this statement in the context of the structural thinness of some markets, particularly in the thin markets of healthcare and social services, where consumer choice is absent or is limited. In this case, nothing of the kind of prosperity that Norman mentions could ensue, whether personal prosperity or societal prosperity.

What are thin markets? In the healthcare sector, as in any other sector where such markets exist, a 'thin market' refers to the existence of a gap or gaps between the needs of consumers and the goods and services that are available to them in that market. There can be many reasons why such market deficiencies exist. It is very apparent in markets that are geographically challenged such as the markets in regional and remote areas. Servicing this market may entail exorbitant costs. Thinness is shown in markets where there is low demand for a particular good or service, and in markets where the consumers are highly dispersed. Thin markets can also exist when the needs of consumers are highly complex such as those in the health and disability sectors, where the complexity of the needs may require specialised resources (e.g. specialised staff to provide services).

Thinness is also seen in markets that are characterized by a high degree of information asymmetry between buyer and seller. Hence, in these thin markets, economic inefficiencies exist. One of the outcomes of economic inefficiency is lack of choice. Consumers in thin markets may have little or no choice over their consumption decisions. When markets are thin, the virtue, value, and morality of a commercial society that Norman highly commends are muted. A fitting example is the disability sector. The thinness of some markets in this sector is proving to be a challenge for the National Disability Insurance Scheme (NDIS), a scheme implemented by the Australian Government with the aim of increasing choice and control for people with a disability over their care and support.

The NDIS was introduced and implemented nationally in July 2016. Intended to support people with significant and permanent disability, the NDIS follows a choice-of-provider model of care, so that those with a disability will have control and independence in the planning and delivery of their care. Giving people with a disability the freedom to choose and to have control over their purchases (the market exchange) is the very essence of NDIS. It is a departure from previous welfare models where people with a disability have little control over the type of support they want and the access to these supports.

Prior to NDIS, a one-size-fits-all approach was adopted. Under this welfare model, block funding was adopted. Block funding refers to non-individualised funds that buy goods and services directly from the provider. This can be in the form of a contract or grant. In short, funding went directly to the provider of goods or services but not directly to the person with a disability. This proved to be problematic in that many services could not respond to the diversity of needs of people with disabilities. The NDIS is aimed at changing this and highlights individualised funding, free market and a neoliberal view of market exchange—an exchange that is based on choice, rights, and freedom to participate.

Norman reminds us that such a system of natural utility is moral. Norman believes that "it gives us what we want, and vastly more . . . it contains a vision of society fit to sustain us in the long-term". But will it really sustain us at all times and in all cases? In the case of NDIS, one size does not fit all. Since its roll-out, the scheme has encountered significant challenges with thin markets. It is well documented that, in these markets, people with a disability have little or have no choice over the planning and delivery of their care.[2] In particular, people with a disability who reside in remote and regional Australia have little or no control over their consumption decisions. The markets are so thin that in some cases, the provision of disability services is non-existent. If services are provided at all, they do have to contend with poor quality care. For the social services sector in general, and the disability sector in particular, the issue is not just about choice. It is not simply a matter of having a choice. It is a matter of having a *meaningful* choice. Any exchange in these thin markets of the disability sector does not result in optimal outcomes because utility maximisation is hindered severely.

Free markets are also grounded on a market structure that favors the availability of competing alternatives. In other words, the presence of competition is a natural offshoot of this free exchange. In thin markets, this important characteristic is either absent or, at the very least, insignificant. Without competing alternatives, no meaningful choice can be made by market participants. Hence, noble as it may seem for the NDIS to aim at improving choice for people with a disability and increasing their control over their own care (which, without question, markets often do very well), the very nature of thin markets impedes their attainment.

In general, the adoption by governments, whether here or abroad, of commercial models of care in the health or disability sector, is driven by efficiency goals. Resources must be used as efficiently as possible. As mentioned, freely functioning markets are highly efficient. Economics reminds us that when we talk about the allocative and economic efficiency of markets then it must be the case that the marginal cost of producing an incremental unit of a good or service is equal to the marginal benefit derived from consuming this incremental unit. In other words, where marginal cost is equal to marginal benefit, the price that the consumer is willing to pay is equal to the benefit or satisfaction (utility) that the consumer derives from the consumption of the good or service. Price is the signaling mechanism in markets. It is also its incentive mechanism. In markets that function freely, prices are free to move reflecting the preferences of independent and free market participants. Due to the nature of thin markets, however, prices do not truly reflect preferences and valuation of consumers. Hence, a commercially-driven model of provision of social services like health and disability services, when implemented in thin markets, raises questions beyond efficiency. In other words, the inefficiency of thin markets in the health and disability sectors may not be the only problem. Here, we are invited to extend our concerns and reflect in the realm of equity and ethics.

The power of markets is beyond dispute. At their best, when

they are fully functioning, they are, highly efficient and effective. As Norman prompts us to see, the exchange of mutual obligations has, time and again, led to beneficial outcomes for both individuals and society. Because it is grounded on individual freedom and the centrality of choice, it is highly moral. Since it assumes that, in the process of freely engaging with markets, individuals make rational decisions to maximise outcomes (the greatest value possible), society is then benefited. Society prospers as a result. This makes a commercial society moral, and it is this morality and virtue that makes it also highly enticing and highly desirable. However, there are markets that are inherently structurally thin. This is best exemplified by the thin markets in the disability sector and the current challenges facing the NDIS. One of the biggest hurdles that the NDIS has to overcome is the thinness of some of the markets in this sector.

To adopt and implement a market-driven model of care in markets that are not conducive to it, or in markets that are not 'market-ready' for such a reform, governments run the risk of counteracting the very nature and intent of a public policy reform, and that is, to achieve the best outcomes possible for the recipients of the reform. The NDIS has been lauded for its intent to increase choice in the marketplace for people with a disability, and thereby address the issues of inequality and lack of access. It may indeed turn out to be persistently inequitable as a scheme, however, unless market gaps and deficiencies such as those posed by thin markets are addressed. Norman talks about the endurance and sustainability of commercial society. However, we must always resolve to find ways to improve or make amends when markets fail.

8

IN PRAISE OF PARTNERSHIP

DAVID CORBETT

When the Stranger says: "What is the meaning of this city?

Do you huddle close together because you love each other?"

What will you answer? "We all dwell together

To make money from each other"? or "This is a community"?

Oh my soul, be prepared for the coming of the Stranger.

Be prepared for him who knows how to ask questions.

T. S. Eliot, *The Rock*

There have been very influential thinkers who have operated on the assumption that the central point of human endeavour is material. Milton Friedman and others on the right have argued that the only purpose of business is "the maximisation of shareholder value". There are strong voices on the left who have argued that the "distribution of the means of production", another economic goal, has always been central to history.

It is unusual that these ideas have been taken so seriously, as any period of short reflection would arouse a clear thought in most people that, whilst money and material goods are important, to make either of these an ultimate thing impoverishes us. What has been missing in this discourse, however, is someone to explain clearly what drives us and the proper place of markets and economics in our thinking. Dr Norman does an excellent job of just this. Norman adopts Adam Smith's term 'commercial society', carefully preferring it to the more commonly used expression 'capitalism'. There is good reason for this. Whilst it is commonplace today for people to describe Adam Smith as the 'Father of Capitalism', Norman points out that capitalism was not a term used or proposed by Smith.

Norman focuses on other issues, but I think it fruitful here to consider at greater length the origin of the term 'capitalism' and its distinction from 'commercial society'. Norman says that 'capitalism' should be understood as the age that has occurred since the joint-stock company. There is a lot to be said for the idea that the joint-stock company was a landmark in commercial history, facilitating gargantuan endeavours and driving economic growth. Yet, although both the term 'capitalism' and the joint-stock company legislation arose in the mid-eighteenth century, they are best kept distinct because they have different origins.

Contrary to popular belief, Karl Marx invented the term 'capitalism' and this creation has had a profound impact on political debate and modern conceptions of morality. Both of these points are relevant to Norman's lecture and might also provide some context for understanding why Norman's lecture was necessary in the first place.

As all politics and parliamentary debates are a 'war of words', the words we use are important. Unfortunately, words are not like artefacts, frozen in time, preserved under layers of silt, which we can dig up just as they were. Words are more like the tools we inherit from our grandpa which we keep using, but in different ways and for new projects. It is worth discussing how 'capitalism' was originally used so we can get a better understanding of it. There is a reason the term 'capitalism' was originally created and this is somewhat relevant to how we use it now.

Ludwig von Mises, amongst others, has noted that the term

'capitalism' was, for all intents and purposes, coined by Marx.[1] Though Marx called it "the capitalist mode of production", one of his acolytes, most likely Max Weber or Werner Sombart, introduced the shorthand 'capitalism' to refer to the same idea.[2] Some confusion has arisen because 'capitalism' was used before Marx by William Makepeace Thackeray to mean something else. There is even a longer provenance of the term *capitaliste* in French. However, a recent study has found Marx to be the most cited scholar of all time,[3] so it is not far-fetched to say that Marx's meaning of the word 'capitalism' has become the dominant meaning of the term. Marx remains the Great Labeller. When we today call ourselves a capitalist society, or speak of today as the age of capitalism, this is because of Karl Marx. Some readers will already be seeing that it is unusual that people on the right gleefully call themselves capitalists. This curiosity is the subject of this essay.

Marx was not only the Great Labeller, but also the Great Framer. He used his idea of capitalism (or, in his longer title, "the capitalist mode of production") as a counterpoint to his vision of a communist society. This is more than just a clever false dichotomy, but something which goes deep into his unique way of seeing the world. Marx developed a theory he called dialectical materialism. This was his view that history always moves forward by the struggle between two disputing economic groups ('classes'). Marx took the idea of historical dialectic from his tutor, the great philosopher G. W. F. Hegel, who argued that history advances by the tension between dual opposing ideas, and then applied Hegel's idea to economics. In our age, Marx says, the historical debate is a struggle between capitalists and workers. Marx sees history and economics as the same thing. He maintains that we must, therefore, choose either capitalism or communism. Marx's frame is alive today when people reject any critique of the economic status quo, what they now understand to be 'capitalism', as just 'communism' (or sometimes 'socialism'—which they perceive to be the weaker term).

Unfortunately, Marx's rhetoric of history as a duel between two opposing forces fitted snugly on the 'left versus right' divide of politics; a divide that had emerged in politics only a generation earlier, in the French Revolution's aftermath. It came to give this new left-right divide its key operating language, so much of politics since Marx has been conceived of as a debate between capitalism and communism.

A problem with the prominent notion that politics is a debate between capitalism and communism is that it introduces material essentialism, which says that the most important questions are economic. Capitalism and communism have one thing in common: they both think the most important thing in life is material; in other words, what capitalism and communism have in common is their materalism. Indeed, Marx said that *the* driving force of history was economics. In his tome, *Das Kapital*, he writes, "it is the ultimate aim of this work to lay bare the economic law of motion of modern society".[4] It is hard to conceive of a statement that more clearly argues that the main questions are economic. However, there is much more to life—and history—than the economic, or the market, to use Smith's term. It is leaving these issues out which has been a major shortfall of modern political debate. What is often missed, however, is that this is because of the influence of Marx.

The most significant response to Marx's two-sided capitalism-communism frame has been not to reject it, and all of its strange presuppositions, but instead to agree with its major premises that the core political question is a choice between the systems of capitalism and communism. The modern right, then, has simply had to discredit communism for capitalism to reign supreme. They have achieved this by pointing to the violence and penury which often comes from Marxist regimes, and the comparative wealth that they attribute to capitalism. Indeed, without even showing exactly how capitalism has produced this, they just point out that it is 'not communist'.

Perhaps the worst, and most insidious, result of Marx's capitalist-communist framing of our politics has been to diminish anything that is not economic. In this way of looking at the world, just about anything that increases wealth is redefined as moral. An iconic person who recaptured the term 'capitalism' for the right was Ayn Rand. She wrote very influential works such as *Capitalism: The Unknown Ideal*. Alan Greenspan, the longest serving Governor of the Federal Reserve, wrote the foreword to this book and took its ideas to heart. Tellingly, Rand also released a book on the morality of capitalism called, *The Virtue of Selfishness*. In this work, Rand outlines her 'moral' framework, but even its title clearly signals she wants to twist traditional categories of morality as selflessness has almost always been seen as a moral virtue. In this book she argues that self-centredness is good, as it *drives* capitalism. This idea was immortalised in the film, 'Wall Street' in the immortal line, "Greed—for lack of a better word—is good". Rand's libertarianism is a response to Marxism, but accepts Marxism's major premise and puts economics at the centre of life. The result of libertarianism's response to Marx is something partly true. Whilst it is better not to have communism, that does not necessarily make it true that it is better to have capitalism, which libertarians regard as the mutually exclusive and jointly exhaustive opposite of communism. Marx's framing of politics as a simple choice between capitalism and communism has had a peculiar effect on our discourse—but also on our understanding of morality. Adam Smith had a different view of markets and morality, which we are now rediscovering, thanks in part to excellent scholars such as Jesse Norman.

Adam Smith had a very strong interest in morality. For him, morality was almost aligned with the purpose of life itself. Smith published two major works, the first was *The Theory of Moral*

Sentiments and the second—more famous—work was *The Wealth of Nations*. While Rand outlined her (im)moral thought in *The Virtue of Selfishness,* Smith provides an extended discussion of the origins and sources of moral thinking in *Moral Sentiments*. Like Rand's, it was published just a few years before his economic work, and in it Smith identifies the core of morality in the avoidance of shame. It is worth highlighting, in the context of Norman's lecture which emphasises the importance of social capital, that shame is a fundamentally social sentiment—as it comes from the opinions of others. Shame therefore requires other people, community, or 'social capital' to use the modern phrase, to function. For shame to operate, we must first know and relate to other people, and as directly as possible.

Smith saw community as a social infrastructure within which commerce can function. It is for this reason that Smith, unlike capitalists and communists, keeps economics and morality separate. He sees them as interrelated and side-by-side, but distinct, perfectly encapsulated by his compound noun 'commercial society' which keeps the economic-materialist-commercial and the social-moral-society distinct. According to this theory, groups of people, or small societies, create the circumstances within which markets, and commerce, can smoothly run.* So how do we create that social infrastructure? The answer, I believe, to building up

---

* The only quotation from Smith that many people know is that "it is not from the benevolence of the butcher, the brewer, or the baker that we expect our dinner, but from their regard to their own interest". This has been egregiously ripped out of context by those seeking to promote 'self-interest' as an alternative basis for commerce. It is worth noting this is the only time 'self-interest' is mentioned by Smith. Smith devoted considerable effort to dissuading readers from accepting the idea that selfishness is a possible basis for society. Smith described as 'licentious' Bernard Mandeville's 1724 work, *Fable of the Bees,* which praised selfishness as creating public benefit from private vice. In many ways, Mandeville's work is a progenitor of libertarianism. In contrast, it is apparent that such an approach to self-interest is inconsistent with Smith's corpus, in which he always saw morality as crucial to tempers and shaping self-interest. His point was that, within the context of a moral society, even self-interest is directed towards mutual benefit. He was using this quote to argue for a moral basis for commercial society, not against it.

social capital is to build up partnerships, in the various realms of life where they are appropriate. It is worth looking first, however, at that darling of the market, its *sine qua non*, the contract.

A contract is a voluntary agreement for a commercial purpose. Norman points out that the law of contract allowed a major advance from pre-commercial society, in which individuals were bound to their feudal lord sometimes involuntarily through ancestral agreements. Norman brilliantly points out this huge advance in his lecture. The inaugural PM Glynn Lecturer, J. D. Heydon, has recently gone even further in his new tome, *Heydon on Contract*.[5] His preface favourably cites Freidrich Hayek's proposition that an effective law of contract is the factor which made the greatest contribution to the prosperity of the West. So contracts are important. However, Norman correctly points out that there are limits to contract.

Contracts are voluntary commercial agreements between people, and are the essence of the market. However, the market is also embedded within a network of social relationships. This network of social relationships, sometimes measured by social capital, engenders moral goods such as trust, which in turn facilitate the market. For example, as contracts are also just an exchange of promises, where there is no trust contracts will breakdown. However, social relationships are the purpose of the market, rather than just the infrastructure that allows markets to operate. As the epigraph to this essay reminds us, the purpose of society is not just to get rich, but to foster society—and its relationships—as an end in itself. That is why we "huddle together" into a society.

Partnership is primarily about relationship, not just about the economic output created by that arrangement. In partnership, the two parties are in it together: they combine their resources, talents, and interests in ways such that it is hard to distinguish what one person is doing from the other. However, this relationship is unnecessary to a contract and they are theoretically kept relationally distant ('at arm's length'). These long-term relationships, or partnerships, are the relationships which in turn constitute society. It is not by coincidence the term 'society' is derived from a Latin word for partnership.[6]

The important distinction between contracts and partnerships is that contracts are market-interactions and partnerships do not have to be engaged with the market. Any relationships involved in contract are incidental to its commercial purpose and are often transactional and short-term. However, partnerships are often longer-term—even life-long in the case of marriage. Partnerships can exist within markets, but share many of the characteristics of non-market social relationships: genuine warmth, long-term commitment, fellow-feeling. Partnership-relationships are relationships which may venture into the market but are not defined by the market.

There are, of course, some not strictly voluntary arrangements which are necessary for a society to work outside contracts and partnerships. Sometimes these involuntary partnerships are called 'institutions', which Edmund Burke was right to revere.[7] One of them is parliament, which is essential to the context within which markets, and therefore commercial life, can operate. There are also associations, which are groupings for purposes other than profit. These are fertile grounds for relationships but they cease when the common activity ends, whereas a partnership can move between activities as the relationship is not determined by the common activity. Institutions and associations are also important, but I think the area that has been most overlooked today is partnership.

Between contracts and institutions sits this area of partnership. Partnership agreement is by 'covenant', not contract. The distinguishing feature is that a contract requires a commercial element (consideration) to be binding, whereas a covenant does not. For Christians, covenant is a rich concept. A Christian's covenant with God is the basis of his or her freedom. Christians see themselves as free, not in the sense of being free *from* other people, but in the sense of being free *to* partner with and serve who they like, and the longer those relationships endure, the more intimate and meaningful they often become. The heart of a Christian's life is the relationship which he or she chooses to make with God. The covenant between God and the Christian is the basis of the Christian's freedom. The sense of service and mutual warmth that partnerships engender in a society creates the social infrastructure within which a market can operate meaningfully, and also effectively.

It is the partnerships in a society which make it function. In the domestic sphere, it is the marriage between two individuals from which a new a family starts. From this partnership, the next generation is reared; a precondition to any economic life and market. There are partnerships which operate in the transactional sphere, but they themselves are partnerships to add a solidity to their function: for example, equity partnerships in law firms. However, forgetting how to structure partnerships has meant that in today's law firms, so-called 'partners' often function more like competitors. This is a big problem for society as the relationship between partners is the way in which they are supposed to socially-regulate. The old mutuals, which share some features of associations, began with a form of partnership where people banded together for mutual self-help and formed a 'friendly association'. In recent decades, these friendly societies have between dismantled in a process called 'demutualisation' and turned into 'insurance corporations'. Mutuals were a benefit to a society as they reduced reliance on the state for welfare. There are also other forms of partnerships that recognise the shortcomings of the market in their particular context, such as cooperatives, in which people band together to make the market work in the interest of them together, rather than as individuals, e.g. farmers' cooperatives to reduce the cost of production. Importantly, these are citizen-initiated rather than government-enforced endeavours, unlike communist equiv-alents. Partnerships are a marvel that should be given a renewed focus so that Adam Smith's commercial society can flourish.

In regard to marriage partnerships, the words of the Book of Common Prayer said marriage was designed (by God) for "mu-tual society, help, and comfort". This arrangement was not first about money, or even children. And one of its core purposes was to stop loneliness—mutual society may even have been the core purpose for marriage.[8] Contrast this with today, when marriage is seen more as a contract that can be ended simply because one per-son is no longer satisfied. It is now as though spouses are dealing with a product, rather than another person. We are, as a society, importing contractual values into non-market realms. It is little wonder that today's society is facing an epidemic of loneliness.

Turning to the legal profession, partnerships were the preferred method of keeping law firms self-regulated for many generations. Partners were mutually responsible for each other's actions and would, therefore, keep an eye on each other's behaviour. They also knew each other well enough to do a good job of it, much better than any government regulator. They had an internal form of social capital. Only in recent decades have law firms moved away from this partnership structure. This breaks down the long-term relationship between partners and as a result the ability for law firms to socially self-regulate.

Insurance organisations started as mutual societies. These were organisations in which people partnered for mutual self-help to guard against the exigencies of life. A mutual was comprised of members; members were simultaneously both customer *and* shareholder. This worked very well for over 150 years. The trial judge in the case against the NRMA's demutualisation observed that the merits of the mutual structure were never challenged.[9] Now that the NRMA is incorporated, there is a fundamental misalignment between customers and shareholders. Rather than banding together to reinvest their profits over the long-term, so that the group can provide practical support for each other if any of them fall on tough times, the interests of the shareholders are often preferenced over and above the interests of the (former) members. This does not work in a structure like insurance, which is at root about a long-term partnership and mutual concern for when the unexpected happens. Not surprisingly, large demutualised organisations, like the AMP, are beginning to fail.

Noel Skelton, a great barrister-statesmen who conceived the original 'property-owning democracy' idea, argued convincingly that partnerships are the answer to Marx's capitalist-communist frame.[10] Unlike those before us, who have allowed Marx's frame to define the debate, we should reject it comprehensively. Otherwise, whenever capitalism struggles, we will hear calls for socialism or communism. Witness the rise of Jeremy Corbyn in Britain. 'Co-partnery', where all members of the businesses are partners in it, resolves Marx's framing problem. Marx sought to split people into two classes, roughly capitalists/bourgeoisie and workers/proletariat. Skelton argued that co-partnery, a partnership between all members of a business, could overcome this. It makes sense. When employees are made part-owners of the business they work in—and not just given a share in its profits (shares) but also a meaningful say in how it is run—they are no longer employees but fellow owners, or in Marx's terminology 'bourgeoisie'. When everyone is an owner, Marx's dialectic disappears. The unnecessary divide between bosses and employees is overcome as all are owners. This is what Skelton meant by the property-owning democracy (not widespread homeownership which the phrase has come to mean). It is true that there will remain a difference in *degree*, as one person may own one share and another one hundred, but the difference in *kind* has disappeared. Marx's class distinction thus loses its meaning, and so does his central argument about how society should change. Employee-partnerships are possible, and often, advisable even on economic grounds. An eminent example is the John Lewis Partnership in Britain. Its long-term success testifies to their practicability. Employee-ownership is a small but burgeoning movement in Australia, and Employee Ownership Australia has demonstrated many benefits even including a significant productivity premium of co-partnered businesses over their peers. So Skelton's suggestion of co-partnery is not just a practical way to overcome Marx's false dichotomy, but also often economically beneficial.

Norman undertook an excellent initiative when he founded the Conservative Cooperative Movement. This existed both to education about the founding of cooperatives, and importantly, to demonstrate that there are more categories to label economic initiatives than just 'capitalist' or 'communist'. This is important, as many people have come to associate cooperatives with the left, whereas they are, in fact, a profoundly conservative idea about building up local communities and individual initiative to reduce the need for government intervention in markets. This form of partnership-style structure is well worth exploring further.

Overall, I think it is fair to say that partnerships are the practical manifestation of society. They serve as a sort of social infrastructure within which commercial society can operate. It is these partnerships we need to explore further to create a fairer and more purposeful nation. However, this will require a lot of dreaming, as we are not accustomed to thinking in this way.

Let us end with a brief coda.

Imagine you are standing at Circular Quay, in the humming heart of Sydney. It's a sunny day, you crane your neck to look up and gaze upon Sydney's first skyscraper—the Australian Mutual Provident Society (AMP) Building—standing tall, proudly representing the hundred years of *mutual* self-help before its demutualisation. A monument to the mateship of days gone by. You squint and see that the building is looking dated—as though it represents an old idea. You remember the demutualisation of the AMP in the late 1990s and lament how this has allowed a mean streak in Australia to come through. One-time members are now divided into shareholders and customers, and recently it was revealed that the business has even begun to steal from those it now calls 'customers' for the benefit of its shareholders.

To take your mind off that, you stroll up the foreshore to the Opera House and take in the dappled sunlight across the water and the two iconic monuments that stand for Sydney to the world: the festoon arch of the Sydney Harbour Bridge and the sails of the Opera House. Remembering that the engineering firm for the Opera House, Arup, is a type of rarely-used partnership model, in which the company is employee-owned and every employee is a partner in the business, having both an owner's say in the running of the firm and its profits. Still existing and growing, it is a heartening reminder that partnerships are still possible. But you wonder why there aren't more.

Turning to the pressing question of how to get back home to Manly, you see two options: the government-run Manly Ferry and the privately-owned fast ferry. The government option takes nearly an hour, but has that form of grandeur reserved for something which has become an institution, even painted in Australian green and gold; the privately-owned fast ferry gets you there in half the time but charges twice as much, and has a cold and anonymous utilitarian aesthetic. Neither seem ideal. That's when you swivel on your heel and take a new direction. You walk halfway to Circular Quay and pop down to an often-missed small wharf there. You step onto the back of a smaller, lovely traditional boat: emblazoned across the back is *The Mateship*. You don't pay because you are a part-owner and you greet Rob and Jess, your fellow Manly-siders on the 5.30pm. Knowing them well, you have a warm conversation on the way home. A welcome relief from the internationalist monotony of the international corporation you work for. The boat pulls straight into Skiffies, the local sailing club your boat cooperative runs out of, and you see others also having a drink, some with their children in tow. You sit down to have a beer and talk further with your companions. You feel like you have left the market behind, over the water, and have stepped into a different sphere of social life; a space away from the marketplace.

We need to rebuild a society that the market has diminished; one that has the freedom of commerce and the morals of society. Dr Norman has shown us the broad philosophy. Now it is up to us to breathe life into it.[11]

9

OF BOSSINESS AND LEADERSHIP

PARNELL PALME MCGUINNESS

A terrible thing has happened to leadership. Modern management culture has co-opted the notion to gloss up corporate bureaucracies and glorify the act of bossing about people who are paid to be bossed.

An equally terrible thing has happened to democracy. It bought into that managerial notion of leadership. But management and leadership are fundamentally different things. They can co-exist, but do not necessarily. Conflating them has done mischief to business. Now, in an era of political professionalisation, it is ripping apart the fabric of democracy.

Edmund Burke reminded the electors of Bristol that he owed them his judgement, not his obedience—he had, he said, been chosen as a representative, not an executive. The difference between representative and executive in Burke's conception is one of empowerment, a vesting of trust. The representative is chosen for qualities that go beyond the ability to execute the will of the people; he is expected to make wise decisions that go beyond individual or even regional interests. This locates the 'we' of politics at the level of the nation as a whole, as Dr Jesse Norman puts it. Because "the purpose of politics is not to satisfy the felt needs of any individual or generation; it is to preserve and enhance the social order in the national interest". This notion of representation transcending individual, regional, or even generational needs, based on trust and held for as long as that trust can be maintained, is leadership as the Bible conceives it. Though he did not, and would not, have compared himself to a biblical figure, this is the idea of the leader as a shepherd of men.

It is an understanding of leadership that was once embraced, subsequently misused, and now largely lost.

Yet the Australian Leadership Index produced by Swinburne University recently found that Australians still subscribe to it. The Index reports that "from a community perspective, leadership for the greater good occurs when leaders demonstrate high ethical standards, when they demonstrate transparency and accountability for their positive and negative impacts, and when they seek to balance the interests of multiple stakeholders, including the wider community in which their institutions are nested". Only two percent of survey respondents believed the chief focus should be "creating positive economic outcomes". However, we should not interpret this to mean that people are not interested in economic outcomes. Rather, it reflects the fact that economic outcomes are produced in a social context—a sentiment very much in line with Norman's observation that "markets and morals cannot be separated from each other, for both rely on the human capacity for empathy and exchange". Economics is not, and could never be, a value-free science.

If a leader owes no obedience, he or she also cannot insist on obedience in the way a manager can. Which is why leadership should not be conflated with the management of paid underlings. A leader is a leader only as long as others choose to follow. When followers withdraw their trust; when they are no longer persuaded by the vision and direction of the leader, the leader ceases to be a leader. The role of leader cannot be bestowed via promotion. There is a power balance of a kind, between the leader and the follower, who can withdraw support at any time. To follow someone is a choice; to become a leader is not. When we lament a lack of leadership, it is because they see no-one worth following.

The dearth of leadership seems to be the result of a lack of purpose, or clear mission among those seeking to be leaders. I conduct a little test on young political hopefuls, whenever they stray across my path. I ask them why they want to be in politics. Nine times out of ten the answer is "to make a difference". Further enquiry is futile. Too few can articulate exactly what difference they want to make or what unique value they will add. Young Liberals will often also say something to the effect that they believe in supporting business and the free market, which is a curious response from someone who has participated in neither. Young Labor want to help people—increasingly, people they have never met and who have no interest in the type of help they are offering.

It would not matter, except that politics has become a career path. There is a good chance some of those political hopefuls will end up in parliament without any experience of the real world.

In the forty-third parliament, forty percent of MPs were previously political consultants, advisers, lobbyists, party administrators, unionists, members of state or territory legislatures, or public servants. The most common recruitment ground for those roles is student politics and party youth wings. The *Griffith Review* essay series on "Fixing the System" adds:

> To the extent that we read about diversity in the backgrounds of MPs in their parliamentary biographies, such career markers have been strategically embarked on for the purpose of a future tilt at politics; for appearance rather than life experience. Too many MPs with backgrounds in larger organisations have worked within the media or government affairs divisions, rather than at the heart of the business.

There are three observations to make about this. First, those involved in politics from an early age have contact primarily with other political animals rather than 'normal' people, limiting their experience of real-person concerns. Secondly, drawing your salary from the public purse or a large corporation means never experiencing a boss who is struggling to balance the books and pay you at the end of the month—and certainly never being responsible for managing cashflow yourself. Thirdly, the people who rise through this system do so by being agreeable to their peers in politics, not by presenting a vision that goes beyond politics.

They are not equipped to become leaders, because they have nothing to lead on. At best this system can turn out competent managers for whom, as Norman says, "election is the goal rather than the means of achieving goals".

The rise of 'populist' minor parties has coincided with an increasing distaste for career politicians. These brand-new parties emphasise that their candidates are 'real' people. Losing this precious realness can cost support. When representatives of Pauline Hanson's One Nation were caught on camera touting for foreign donations in return for influence over Australia's gun laws, support for her party halved. On the other hand, when Donald Trump was accused of doing property deals overseas while campaigning to be president, his fan base were not troubled. He was acting like a real person stumbling into politics; she was acting like a political party pretending to be of the people.

This is not a logical or especially useful development in politics. There is no guarantee that every real person who gets a leg-up from a minor party will be a leader, and many are not. Ricky Muir, a Victorian Motoring Enthusiast Party candidate elected to the Senate on preferences was clearly not. He was unable to find a purpose or a constituency, made barely a ripple, and was unable to maintain his place in the Senate at the 2019 election.

Nonetheless, if the major parties are to fix what ails them, they will have to embrace people with life experience and purpose beyond politics. More importantly, it would be both right and expedient to limit themselves to a more moderate number of careerists in order to get elected. This will be easier said than done. It is easy to point to someone else who should sacrifice their ambitions for the good of the party, less appealing to do so yourself; easy to finagle your way to becoming the notional leader of a faction than to become a leader of people.

Unfortunately for many who seek it, purpose, like inspiration, does not always arrive on cue. The thirty-sixth President of the United States, Lyndon B. Johnson, was one of the few who managed to transcend his own ambitions to become, for a while at least, a genuine leader. In her book tracing the leadership of several American presidents, Doris Kearns Goodwin relates how assiduously LBJ climbed the greasy pole, including being elected President following the Kennedy assassination. Whilst President, he suffered a serious heart attack, fell into a depression and began to wonder what it had all been for:

> He had laid the foundation of a substantial fortune, but what purpose did that wealth serve? He had learned to manipulate the legislative machine of the Senate with a deftness without parallel in American history. But to what end? What large and lasting benefit to the people at large had issued from such an accumulation of power?

It was this contemplation that led him back to the values that originally attracted him to public service—"the idea that government should be used to help those who needed help: people of colour, the elderly, the sick, the undereducated, the ill-housed"—and turned him into a leader. For the brief period of his presidency during which he proceeded with purpose, he achieved strides in civil rights, education, and health.

While LBJ inspired himself by thinking of others, he inspired others to follow him. But when he was unable to locate a purpose higher than management, the people lost faith. He had no conviction in handling the Vietnam War, no vision to guide the country in this difficult endeavor, writes Kearns Goodwin. His period of leadership was subsumed. He is remembered by many as the President who betrayed the American people by conducting a protracted, bloody, and ultimately futile struggle.

The centrality of purpose emerges as the lesson of the life and leadership of Edmund Burke, who, Norman says, "was devoted to an ideal of public duty, and deplored the tendency to individual or generational arrogance". Burke "tempts us to the heretical thought that the route to a better politics may not be through managerial claims—'we can do it better'—but through a deep change of viewpoint." He "offers principles that do not change, the sanction of history and the moral authenticity of those willing to give up power to principle. He gives us again the lost language of politics: a language of honour, loyalty, duty, and wisdom, which can never be captured in any spreadsheet or economic model."

This is the principle of small-c conservatism, not the didactic moralising of the public Conservative. It is the ability to seek to improve and progress, whilst always valuing that which exists.

It might be too late to undo the damage that management theory has done to business leadership, now that there are schools and journals devoted to the perpetuation of the debased concept of the executive-leader. But as liberal democracies search for a way to maintain legitimacy in the face of waning trust, understanding leadership as earned, purposeful, and temporary is central to restoring humility to a gift which confers power in the present and a responsibility for generations to come.

Burke promised the electors of Bristol that he would exercise his judgement humbly, valuing what society had built. It proved to be a vision of such profundity that he became a leader to people around the world. And as long as he has followers, he continues to lead centuries after his death.

10

MORAL RENEWAL AMIDST POLITICAL CHAOS

TOM SWITZER

These are dark days for conservatives. In Australia, notwithstanding the unexpected electoral success on May 18, the federal Liberal Party has increasingly shown signs of severe splintering between the small-l liberal wing and its conservative base. In the Brexit era, the British Tories, which have produced so many of the nation's great prime ministers, have resembled nothing so much as a pub brawl. And notwithstanding Boris Johnson's landslide election victory on December 12, there remain very real tensions between the old Heath and Thatcherite wings of the Conservative party. In America, conservatives are all over the place philosophically: the Reaganite free-market wing is fundamentally at odds with Donald Trump's populism and economic nationalism, with the latter in the political ascendancy.

At the same time, progressive and social democrat parties are lurching further towards the ideological left: from their embrace of divisive identity politics to support for more interventionist economic policies in the name of reducing inequality. Jeremy Corbyn, Bernie Sanders, and to a lesser extent, Bill Shorten all represent this wave of thinking.

When I put it to Jesse Norman on my Radio National program last April that conservatism was in crisis, he was circumspect. Politically, yes, broad centre-right coalition parties and movements are showing real signs of fracturing. However, as a set of ideas, conservatism is not in crisis.

So it is not surprising that in his PM Glynn Lecture, Norman goes beyond these widespread contemporary concerns about the splintering of the right and more generally the fracturing of politics in Western democracies. His main focus instead is commercial society, and he brings to this task his background as an academic philosopher, a biographer of Edmund Burke and Adam Smith, and a British parliamentarian who has served under three Conservative prime ministers—David Cameron, Theresa May and Boris Johnson.

As Norman observes, capitalism is frequently blamed for the social ills of declining social mobility, growing divisions between rich and poor, fears about loss of national identity, "and the escalating belief that the basic values of respect, hard work, and public service are being lost in celebrity worship, consumerism, and the money culture".

In a 16 February 2019 leader, *The Economist* noted the resurgence of socialism as a fashionable corrective to the ills of capitalism, "Socialism," it argued, "is back because it has formed an incisive critique of what has gone wrong in western societies. The left has focused on inequality, the environment, and how to vest power in citizens rather than elites."

This is a view held with increasing conviction by so-called 'millennials'—those born between roughly 1982 and 1998—who are generally mistrustful of markets and prefer to see increased levels of public spending funded, in turn, by increased taxation. The error underlying the millennials' point of view, of course, is their focus on the redistribution of wealth rather than the generation of wealth.

As I have often told millennials, you don't tax a loss: you only tax a profit. Without profit—without capitalism—you cannot raise the revenue to provide public healthcare, education, law and order, or defence. There is no economy in history that has benefited from socialism. All economies that have enjoyed sustained growth and have broadened prosperity have done so through free trade and free markets. Or as Margaret Thatcher once observed: "The trouble with socialism is that eventually you run out of other people's money."

A principal challenge for classical liberal think-tanks, such as the Centre for Independent Studies, is to counter effectively the view, especially popular amongst millennials, not only that inequality is increasing, but that the vested interests of the elites are accruing more and more economic might. It is fashionable to attribute responsibility for these developments to free trade and the market economy; but Norman rightly sounds a note of caution.

The socialist vision of the democratised, equalised, heavily regulated economy will never yield prosperity and raised living standards. Collective action sanctioned by the thud of centralised government will stifle rather than stimulate the health of the institutions of civil society. It is these institutions that help foster the spirit of mutual obligation that, in turn, forms the essential moral basis of a commercial society.

The roots of change occurring in the political topography of countries such as the United Kingdom, the United States, and European countries such as France and Hungary lie deeper than economics. Indeed, Norman warns that it is a serious error to assume these changes are attributable to nothing more than economic discomfort. "At root," he states, "they concern basic questions of identity and legitimacy". The answers to these questions can, in turn, inform our understanding of the nature of modern society.

Norman boldly sweeps aside attempts by earlier thinkers—ranging widely from Aquinas to Bentham—to answer these questions of identity and legitimacy. For reasons that Norman gives only in spare terms, neither the natural law tradition nor a Kantian conception of universal duties; neither a Hobbesian concept of a social contract nor utilitarian appeals to maximal happiness can account adequately for the intricate and mutual dependency that characterizes a healthy modern society.

In their place, Norman proposes what he calls "the tradition of natural utility" to explain the nature of modern society. It is a tradition that draws upon the thought of Burke and Smith and so is informed by classical eighteenth-century expositions of individual and economy liberty.

Norman argues that the vitality of human relationships—sustained by bonds of trust and a sense of mutual obligation—is the *sine qua non* of a healthy civil society; but it is a concept eclipsed by a growing preference for state involvement in many Western societies, and for a widening preoccupation with correcting what are perceived to be social and economic inequalities.

Norman is right to acknowledge the importance of Adam Smith for understanding the contemporary economic prosperity of successful modern economies. Smith identified commercial society as the process which has generated great prosperity by means of the creation of substantial ties of economic interdependence. Exchange, trust, and the generation of mutual obligation underpinned the emergence of commercial society.

Critics of the capitalist economy frequently round upon what they condemn as the immorality of the market. They mean by this that the market, as a mechanism of exchange, is indifferent to the moral weight of different commercial outcomes.

But this criticism is misplaced: markets are impartial rather than indifferent; and they depend upon the moral virtues of trust and honesty if they are to function effectively and efficiently. If it makes any sense to speak of the 'morality' of markets, it is because the moral sense that underpins them is created by human interaction.

For Norman, it is Edmund Burke who gives the most authoritative account of the moral foundations of the civil society upon which a modern economy depends. This foundation comprises all the institutions of civil society—ranging from the government to the legal system; from the press to the voluntary association (comprising the 'little platoons' bound by shared interests). These institutions—the ties that bind, as it were—give shape to every facet of life and social engagement.

Norman's use of Burke here is entirely appropriate as a disposition and framework for reviewing the role of the state. Conservatism, properly understood in the Burkean sense, is anti-doctrinaire. Temperament trumps dogma; and, for conservatives, the single best test of temperament is one's attitude towards change. They are wary of change, and overwhelmingly hostile to sudden radical change—conscious that it can lead to loss as well as gain and is fraught with the danger of unintended consequences. As the prominent Australian conservative Owen Harries once argued: "Discrimination in terms of circumstances trumps consistency in terms of principle and logic, and insistence on consistency regardless of circumstances and consequences is likely to be disastrous."[1]

Another point that Norman correctly brings to the fore is that the institutions and bonds of civil society cannot be imposed or enforced by the state. Rather, each evolves in its own way and at its own pace; and each is, as Norman notes, "a largely accidental and historically contingent human achievement". The social norms of behaviour generated by the bonds forged in civil society underpin exchanges in the market place which generate prosperity and wealth.

How, then, are we to understand the *moral basis of a commercial society*?

Norman answers this question by bringing together the thought of Burke and Smith. Each of them, in their respective analyses of society, shows how the norms of social and economic behaviour generate "habits, practices, and institutions".

We need to recover a strong sense of each of these and to recall that the moral health of the commercial society depends on what Norman correctly identifies as "the human capacity for empathy and exchange." This task of moral renewal is set to become ever more pressing if an effective case is to be made for the moral and economic superiority of capitalism and commercial society.

11

QUESTIONS FOR THE ACADEMY IN AUSTRALIA

TANIA ASPLAND

Morality, commercialism, democratic values, and modern society are key concepts that currently pervade contemporary news bulletins across Australia as freedom of the press, whistle-blowing, and national security come under intense scrutiny. One social media outlet reports: "Very few Australians realise that free speech in this country isn't really a thing. It is not merely not protected— it's far worse than that. If you read any of the vast array of laws that protect government secrets, disclosure in the public interest is discouraged, criminalised, punished, and deplored."[1] The former High Court judge Michael Kirby spoke openly on national television asserting that Australia has very little protection around free speech in comparison to Western allies.[2] The extended debates across all media outlets both nationally and internationally are raising questions about the moral basis of this so-called modern democratic society: Australia. The current situation has been exacerbated by the 'sacking' of a star rugby player in Australia and the negating of his lucrative contract with a large football corporation based on an alleged breach of respectful behaviour. The player is striking back with legal action that claims his dismissal reflects a disregard for his rights to religious freedom in a democratic nation. What we are witnessing in Australia is not unique; it can be identified in most Western nations as conservative governments struggle to find a balance between rights, morality, commercialism, and the core values that underpin humanitarian societies. These debates together with many other similar discussions provide an evidence base that Australia has become, in Jesse Norman's words, "gripped by a kind of moral panic about the nature of modern society."

Cohen, the late South African sociologist, in theorising moral panic, highlights the potential threat to social norms; threats that are enacted through the power plays amongst the media, the policymakers, and the nation state as moral panic evolves within the broader contexts of community.[3] While those in power stand to gain the most from moral panic according to Cohen, it can only be promulgated through the complex interplay of media, authority figures such as police, politicians, and the public; a complex interplay that is "not simply a response to moral panic but part of a circle out of which moral panic develops".[4] Norman provides evidence of evolving moral panic in Britain by referring to "culture wars over sexuality and gender" and through more complex and sustained examples such as "an anger at economic and educational division, and what are seen as entrenched and self-selecting elites; in distrust of traditional authority" and in the "suspicion that those in power are distant, unaccountable, and incapable of leadership."

The context in which moral panic evolves can commonly be in times of economic and social crisis when the "landscape of fear" can be conjured up in the media and promulgated by figures of authority, often resulting in policy or legislative change.[5] Massumi, a Canadian philosopher and social theorist, argues that fear production can be the instrument of "commodity capitalism" and the politics of commodification.[6] In a similar manner, Norman argues that societal reaction to moral panic lies at "the feet of free trade and the capitalist system." However, Cohen would argue that moral panic is also a cultural phenomenon:

> Cohen's map of the cultural coordinates of a panic—the mass media, the dramatic element, social unease, a demonised subculture, 'control agents', the aftermath—still has an heuristic relevance far beyond the historical specificity of his initial work.[7]

Norman argues that the complex issues associated with moral panic cannot by referred to as economic causes or as a result of capitalism alone, rather, these complex issues are embedded in the nature of modern society, citizenship, and humanity.

Calling on the works of Edmund Burke and Adam Smith, Norman theorises the nature of modern society through his theory referred to as the "tradition of natural utility". Central to the theory is the concept of "social interaction" as the basis of identity formation, and the creation of social order—"a web of institutions, customs, traditions, habits, and expectations" that guide reason but are grounded in the subjective elements of humanity. The dynamic interactions amongst the institutions, traditions, habits, and expectations create structures and functions implicit in the evolving social order, bringing meaning to individuals, groups, and communities and the nation state—the framing of political modernity. From this perspective, "the social order becomes a repository of shared knowledge and inherited wisdom". But modern society is not just a political entity—it is also a social entity that invites humans to engage socially with one another—"the human self is a social self". As a result, through human interaction itself, values, morals, and social norms are created and realised as central to social order. According to Norman, Smith identifies the significance of mutual interaction and empathy in shaping the moral norms and social norms that underpin the human values and behaviour that ultimately shape "societal habits, practices, and institutions."

Norman concludes that Smith shows us that the interactions

131

within modern society are political, social, inherently moral, and also *commercial*. In modern society, the complexities of human interdependence have become characterized through the discourse of *exchange* of commodities and interpersonal moral obligation in building communities shaped by a socio-economic order. Norman's Smith refers to this as commercial society: "The moral basis of a commercial society lies in the ceaseless exchange of mutual obligations and personal regard." It can be argued that, ideally, as a commercial society becomes more complex, institutional constructs become more sophisticated, society becomes more civilised, the nation state becomes more powerful, and the desire for social order is prioritised. As Norman points out, however, such idealism can, in some cases, be exploited by those with "ill-intent".

It is significant to note that despite this historically situated theorising about the moral basis of a commercial society, and the argument that social order is a political, cultural, and social construct, based on the early thinking of Burke, Norman recognises "a need to preserve a sense of the divine . . . something that gives a higher meaning and a moral perspective to human lives." This implies that the commercial society is not one that is value free. Rather, "it reminds us that markets and morals cannot be separated from one another."

As a university academic working in a Catholic context, there are some significant points of both connection and concern between Norman's theorising about the moral basis of a commercial society and the context of universities in Australia in contemporary times.

- First, in the Catholic university sector, morals, values, and commercial markets are inextricably intertwined and embedded in a discourse of human capacity-building through the exchange of goods namely, knowledge, dispositions, and capacities;

- Secondly, political and educational leadership in the Catholic university sector must necessarily be guided by moral leadership, to preserve the traditional social order of a large religious, educational organisation in the public interest and for the purposes of the common good, albeit it is enacted in a commercial world of marketing, designed primarily to ensure economic and corporate success in a highly competitive industry. Leaders in universities also uphold a cultural responsibility in building an equitable and collaborative community of scholars;
- Thirdly, central to the university sector is the concept of capital; intellectual capital, socio-cultural capital, and political capital.

This third point is one of the greatest concerns for academics working in universities in the Western world. Norman's word of caution that his idealistic thinking about the moral basis of a commercial society can become manifest in challenging ways, is critical at this point. The challenges to universities will be addressed forthwith.

A colleague and I have reported that university governance has been reinvented most recently away from an historical conception of university as "a republic of scholars" to become more closely aligned to a portrayal of the university "as a stakeholder organization".[8] Further, the original twelfth-century purpose of universities as the "emancipatory saviours of societies"—what Norman calls "the 'we' of politics"—has been challenged within the university context by increasing "market regulation" and compliance requirements.[9] One could argue that currently this is the dominant discourse shaping university business in Australia; a discourse that reflects Norman's empty "economic materialism". This shift in focus raises serious questions about the place of the university academic in contributing to social and public good. Further, concerns have been raised about the type of morally neutral leadership that is emerging within the university due to economic rationalist demands that are reconfiguring governance and regulation of universities in Australia.[10] What is emerging is the co-existence of a number of binaries that result in continuing sets of tensions and dilemmas, and what I suggest could be perceived as "moral crises" within leadership in the higher education sector.[11] For example:

- On the one hand, the university professes to uphold the academic freedom of intellectuals to generate knowledge for the betterment of society, which, in Norman's words, helps to "preserve and enhance social order in the public interest"; while, on the other hand, government regulators allocate funding according to politically motivated national priorities, reflecting a commitment to Norman's "private freedoms rather than a free and educated public realm" that is arguably found in equitable educational opportunities;

- On the one hand, universities profess to develop a desire for learning across a diverse community of students—which arguably aids Norman's aspiration for increasing prosperity and freedom, while, on the other hand, poor university funding constrains innovative and pedagogically advanced engagement in learning supposedly in the interests of nationalism, and in so doing, restricts the university's capacity to enhance what Norman might be thought to have in mind when he talks about "human capabilities and their free expression"; and

- On the one hand, universities are considered the hub of intellectual creativity and forums for the production of new and significant knowledge, which, Norman says, should be "supported by the allegiance of citizens", while, on the other hand, the introduction of mandated national discourses of regulation have resulted in an ethos of compliance across the sector that stifles innovation, limits pedagogical engagement, and necessarily becomes performance oriented to ensure ongoing funding, reflecting, in words Norman takes from Burke, "setting up trade without capital".

The question of significance at this point is: In the emerging context of regulation, compliance, marketisation, and economic rationalism in higher education, what type of leadership is required? More fully, what catalyst is required in universities to influence the reform that Norman proposes (in relation to political leadership) so that universities, as one of the major social agencies in Australia, are positioned to raise the consciousness of leaders in reshaping the moral underpinnings of the commercial society in ways that influence the preservation and enhancement of Norman's "social order in the public interest". In a Catholic context, where universities engage "in the Catholic intellectual tradition where faith and reason are compatible in education, and knowledge is cultivated in an environment that fosters intellectual freedom, personal development and equity for all", this question is all the more significant.[12]

Traditionally, in universities constrained by market regulation, a top-down governance model of leadership has been evident. This implies that a model of leadership "is exercised when a leader and followers undertake, as it were, a transaction: from the followers, an agreement to work toward the achievement of organizational goals from the leader, an agreement to ensure good working conditions or, in some way, satisfy the needs of followers".[13] An hierarchical structure of accountability is encouraged within this paradigm of compliance, with bonuses and promotions often used by transactional leaders for subordinates who work within organizational expectations and high levels of performance. Burns, an

American historian and political scientist, notes that explicit and implicit contractual relationships are evident in such transactional working culture in organizations and that formal statements about the conditions of employment, rules, regulations, benefits, and disciplinary codes are articulated through performance review policies and procedures.[14]

Kenny, an Australian education expert, along with other scholars, contends that a combination of linear models of management, "tight control over policy, a competitive ethos and the management of academics", along with an alignment to federal funding agencies and "political and bureaucratic priorities" typify current Australian higher education.[15] This highly inflammable potion of corporate priorities in an academic environment gives rise to what could be deemed moral dilemmas or at times, moral panic, enacted as the powerplays emerge amongst the university leaders, the policymakers, academic staff, students, and broader contexts of community. Key among these tensions is the need to strike a balance between compliance and creativity, and to fulfil the academic obligation in leading governance, quality teaching and learning, and research replete with what Norman calls "conversations of civil, honest and independent minds".

Currently, there is evidence in universities of a model of leadership that is shaped by marketisation and is designed to generate wealth and successful economic outcomes for universities in times when funding is being reduced. The moral implications of such leadership behaviour cannot be overlooked. A form of leadership that is shaped by economic rationalist thinking and marketisation is not what Norman looks for in his commercial society; the type of leadership that is prevalent today in universities reflects behaviours that Norman argues, in the context of political leadership, "have been subsumed by hierarchies and structures of an overwhelming collective and goals"; goals that may be deemed morally neutral. In contrast, the concept of leadership that Norman implicitly advocates requires the building of a commercial university profile that "rests on mutual obligation and mutual esteem", it "begins in respect for social order . . . it insists on the common good, and the importance of public service and public duty".

Some experts have argued that administrative structures that are autocratic foster academic incivility and foster power imbalances that leave staff demoralised.[16] Leaders of this autocratic type have been described as self-centred, power-hungry workers who are territorial, highly competitive, challenged by others, and pushed to extremes by a "survival of the fittest mentality".[17] Further, it has been shown that leaders of this type are often rewarded for their leadership prowess in the university.[18] Some time ago,[19] a colleague and I asked the question: How can this be so in the workplace context of higher education, where academic freedom and autonomy are paramount to ongoing scholarship?[20] This question reflects the very point that Norman aspires to in building complex institutions that are integral to a commercial society: "it is time to recognise what matters about the modern era is not so much about capitalism [and economic rationalism] but commercial society itself".

As Norman calls for renewal away from "empty economic materialism", it is timely to rethink a model of leadership that can be introduced into the university context that better supports and facilitates the recognition of moral leadership models that are integral to commercial society itself and central to the modern era of universities. In doing so, a Catholic university can also, as a community, enable people to celebrate their "own religious faith, and to become people of integrity and generosity".[21]

This is a not an easy task in the current context of higher education in Australia. In recent years, a number of moral dilemmas, moral crises, and moral panic have been witnessed. The moral panic can be evidenced, for example, through the ongoing reviews taking place in higher education at this very moment, all funded fully by the government and testimony to the lack of confidence that politicians have in the university sector. Emerging changes in legislation continue to constrain the autonomy of universities in their brief to maintain Norman's "social order [as] a repository of shared knowledge and inherited wisdom". The lack of trust became evident in 2018 when federal politicians became "part of a circle out of which moral panic resulted".[22] All components of Cohen's definition of moral panic could be evidenced at that time:

1. "the mass media sustained the dramatic elements" of the government's mistrust of university leaders and the need for greater regulation of higher education through endless publications highlighting the tensions and alleged failure of universities to provide quality outcomes for the nation;

2. "social unease"—the public became dismayed and worried about the future of their children or themselves as they enrolled in universities and whether costs would continue to elevate as the demand driven system was reviewed and ultimately changed by the government despite university protests;

3. "a demonized subculture" of academic staff, students, and leaders grew out of the disrespect that was vocalised through parliamentary decisions and promulgated further by the media;

4. "control agents" from public, private, and independent agencies contributed to the debate that eventually led to policy and legislative change; and

5. "parliamentary representatives" persisted in claiming authority over the purposes of universities challenging the importance of autonomous governance, national research, and quality teaching and learning.

In the midst of moral panic, it has been perceived by some

commentators that leaders of universities have bunkered down. They have become autocratic in addressing budget cuts and in re-constituting their national and international business interests; in Norman's words, "dominated by norms that were expedient and anti-social". These actions might be deemed by insiders as ex-ploitive and subsumed by hierarchical decision-making and struc-tural reductionist thinking, and, in Norman's words, "designed to usurp and displace the freedoms of commercial society" as well as moral integrity.

In such a context, one can pose the question: what type of leadership is required in universities to facilitate the reform that Norman proposes, and more positively influence and reshape the commercial society and its moral underpinnings? This is a sig-nificant question when considering the importance of the preser-vation and enhancement of "social order in the public interest"—a core objective of legitimate higher education providers in Austra-lia.

The educational literature is replete with suggestions regard-ing a model or models of leadership that might address what is problematic in the university and its purpose to contribute to a commercial society and a moral framing of leadership. Seidman, an American businessman and an advocate for moral leadership, referred to leadership as the business of human endeavour rather than a matter of economics: "At its essence, therefore, business is about human endeavour. And for humans to endeavour together, there must be an animating ethos and ethic of endeavour."[23] He identifies the core challenge as one of trust—amongst all play-ers—difficult in a world of extreme change with no party exempt from moral crises or what follows.

Moral leadership is a model proposed by Seidman in align-ment with many other scholars, particularly leaders working in faith-based or Catholic contexts. Integral to moral leadership are concepts of service, morality, ethics, and community. Moral leadership has also been perceived as leadership practice that is rooted in moral authority.[24]

Seidman elevates the shared purpose of leadership as a mission designed for a journey of trust and hope not one that is centred on outcomes. Humanity is central to leadership decision-making, and governance structures are shaped by collective conversations that reflect empathic listening, truth, courage, and patience. Moral leadership from this perspective is characterised as "wrestling with questions of right and wrong, fairness and justice, what serves others . . . how they impact the greater good".[25] A full expose of the core concepts that underpin the discourse of moral leadership is not relevant here. There is plentiful debate across the field as to how to enact moral leadership for the purpose of moral affirmation.

Recent research introduces the reader to a more complex but similar model of moral leadership entitled "transrelational leadership".[26] This model takes up the key concepts underpinning moral leadership but exemplifies four fundamental principles including:

- The centrality of being an authentic member of the group they are leading;
- Demonstrating the capacity to champion the group;
- Where necessary changing the group's identity to achieve the mission; and
- As an essential responsibility, bringing the external relevant influences to the attention of the group.

What is of significance in the transrelational model is the thought that leadership praxis moves others, the organisation, and the leader to a far more effective level of functioning by means of relationships, not power, not economics nor self-interest.[27]

In response to the question posed earlier as to what type of leadership is required in universities to facilitate the reform that Norman proposes, I would advocate that leadership from a moral or transrelational perspective has great potential to recognise what matters, and to enable what is required to influence and sustain commercial society. Further, this model of leadership has the capacity to confront what is problematic in universities: a form of leadership that reflects behaviours that have been subsumed by hierarchies and structures of overwhelming collective goals; goals that are morally neutral.

It is a matter of urgency that university leaders take heed of the Norman's thinking—at a time of reckoning—to address the moral crises and moral panic that has been experienced in recent years. Universities need to reconstitute the leadership of universities to a form of governance that achieves Norman's standards of being "democratic", able to command the "allegiance of its citizens", and to regain the "legitimacy it has held for centuries" as a republic of scholars (and as Staub's "emancipatory saviours of societies").[28] The introduction of moral leadership and transrelational leadership provides an opportunity to do so. As a result, leaders both political and university-based, may bring hope to higher education and in Norman's words, to "be worthy of admiration of others in the future". More importantly, university leaders may become more enabling in recognising that what matters about the modern era is not so much about capitalism (economic rationalism, profit margins, student enrolments), as commercial society itself.

12

COMMERCIAL SOCIETY AND THE JACOBINS

M. A. CASEY

The idea of the commercial society is Jesse Norman's proposal for averting a new age of Jacobinism;* for forestalling a new chapter in the long era of ideology which commenced with the French Revolution.[1] Common to ideology in all its forms is the conviction that what is problematic in the human condition is precisely the human, and that solutions to particular problems or evils can really only be attained by escaping from it, either entirely or in part. In its milder democratic forms, ideology is characterised more by impatience with the human condition, while in its more extreme forms contempt and hatred would be the appropriate words. The specific objects of these powerful emotions—the things that get in the way of a clean sweep—are, however, largely the same: our attachments to family and friends, to locality and the environment around us, to habit, custom, and country; the persistence of religious faith or benighted ideas of politics, the economy, morality,

---

* A Jacobin was a member of the Jacobin Club, established in Paris in 1789, originally as a club for members of the Third Estate to discuss legislative strategy. The Jacobins established a formidable political machine, with affiliates across France, and became the most radical and ruthless of the political groups formed in the wake of the French Revolution. In association with Robespierre they instituted the Terror of 1793-94. 'Jacobinism' continues to be used by contemporary political commentators to denote political ideologies of an extremely radical nature. As François Furet has noted, "by way of bolshevism, the Jacobin party enjoyed an illustrious twentieth century".

and the order of things; the preference we give to the interests of ourselves, those closest to us, and the community in which we live; our wilfulness and ignorance in insisting on thinking for ourselves and refusing to adhere to things we do not believe.

Depending on innumerable conditions of choice and circumstance, these and the many other attributes of human experience can result in peace and flourishing, weariness and vexation, or horror, sorrow, and despair. In his lecture, Norman presents commercial society as one way of working with, rather than against, the attributes that belong to us as human beings in pursuit of peace and flourishing. Opposed to this is an ideological approach which, with some warrant from Norman himself, we can appropriately describe as Jacobinism. In speaking of the importance of social capital, he quotes Edmund Burke's rebuke to the English Jacobins: they "began by despising everything that belonged" to them, and with the arrogant conceit that they "had everything to begin anew". Whatever specific form it may take today, these remain the fundamental features of Jacobinism: contempt for the condition that belongs to us as embodied creatures embedded in relationships and communities, and the overwhelming desire to extirpate us from this condition so that things may be utterly new.

The foundation of Norman's concept of commercial society is the humanness of the human condition. Following Adam Smith, he argues that social norms arise from our social nature, that their origin lies in ourselves as "being[s] whose nature is to be in society". This sociability itself is a function of our interdependence; our need for each other. It is this interdependence which generates the dynamics of economic exchange at the heart of commercial society, whereby people seek to better their condition on the basis of reciprocity and imaginative identification with the needs and aspirations of others. Reciprocity—taking on obligations to each other—and imaginative identification are not, however, confined to a utilitarian process of exchange to secure what we need to survive and prosper economically. It is also in our nature to watch each other's actions, to form judgements about them, and to conform our own conduct to these judgements, mindful that we ourselves are being observed and judged according to our actions by others.

This concern for judgement and conduct goes far beyond how we are regarded by others for the purposes of trade and exchange. It is not sufficient for human beings merely to be thought reliable and honest so that others might do business with us or give us employment (though no doubt there are some who are happy to settle for this). For the most part, we seek "not only to be admired but to be worthy of the admiration of others"—not least of all in our own eyes. Norman quotes Smith to underscore this point: we seek "not only to be loved, but to be lovely; or to be that thing which is the natural and proper object of love".

Smith and Norman have something here. While we are more than willing to trade in counterfeits and to deceive ourselves and others in all manner of ways for all manner of reasons, there is nevertheless deep within us some irreducible and inescapable impatience with appearance alone, and all the more so when we suspect that the appearance before us is false. Human beings are creatures who want the real thing, from others certainly, but perhaps even more so in one's own self as well. Admiration of goodness in another, for example, is based on a judgment that this person is in reality good. This is not just a judgement based on the satisfaction that may be given by a pleasing appearance of goodness. For this reason, the person judged to be good, and admired by others as such, may not value this so highly if, in his own estimation of himself, he falls short of the mark. Even at the level of exchange, to say nothing of the larger life in common of which exchange is a part, there is too much at stake to be satisfied by mere appearance.

In Norman's summary of Smith's sociology, "mutual interaction and empathy" become "the basis for moral norms", and "once a norm is established—be it a moral norm of personal integrity and truth-telling, or a social norm of good manners and fair dealing, it takes on a life of its own and becomes authoritative to others". The "ceaseless exchange of mutual obligations and personal regard" is the moral basis of a commercial society, creating "wealth and the benefits of economic order" in markets, and "ethical and social norms of behaviour" for society more broadly. These in turn generate "habits, practices, and institutions" which humanise social life and restrain the exercise of state power, making for a life in common which is at once orderly and dynamic, fostering at the same time human capabilities and freedom, together with tolerance, mutual respect, and moderation.

Norman draws on Edmund Burke to explain how social order is sustained in the midst of the ceaseless movement and innumerable interactions that constitute human social life. The critical point is that this order is neither static nor rigid. It comprises instead an "ever-shifting web of institutions, customs, traditions, habits, and expectations". Institutions are particularly important here because they "trap and store knowledge", the knowledge yielded by custom, tradition, habit, and expectations, each of which itself is a form of learning and experience. In this, institutions serve as "stores of memory and politics . . . channels for the articulation and reconciliation of conflicting views and interests . . . [a] national treasury of shared history and self-understanding" which it is the responsibility of political leaders to bring to life and deploy as a resource and guide for meeting the challenges of the day.

The role of institutions in social order is quite tangible and practical. Among the functions that Norman highlights is the way they constrain other institutions and the institutions of the state, "competing and co-operating as required", and diffuse power "across communities". Another important function is the way they make it possible for people to hold together "overlapping identities and personal loyalties, giving "shape and meaning" to their lives and "rhythms to the day or year". Institutions "are ultimately grounded in feeling and emotion, which guide and direct man's reason", and are "bound together by affection, identity, and interest".

Norman acknowledges that institutions can take anti-social forms "such as cartels and gangs" and emphasises that the idea of the commercial society is not a panacea. He also highlights how the outward forms of a society may remain but be "subsumed by the hierarchies and structures of an overwhelming collective goal". Ideological formations such as these which displace "the equal status and freedoms implicit in the idea of a society"—Norman describes them as "enforced communities"—falsify both social order and the idea of a life in common. They debase "the ceaseless exchange of mutual obligations and personal regard" on which a genuine society depends and turn social life against itself.

In a short space in his PM Glynn Lecture, Norman provides a very rich account not only of the idea of commercial society, but of what makes any form of genuinely human society tolerably human. The essential virtues and attributes can be listed easily: sympathy, empathy, or some form of imaginative identification with others; interaction with people as a necessary condition of society, as a natural constant, carried out usually in a frank and more or less good-mannered way; a basic integrity of process and procedure in economic and other areas of public life, together with a generalised esteem for integrity in personal life; an assumption that telling the truth is usually the norm, not the exception, all things being equal, and that there is something wrong in lying or misrepresenting the truth; and reciprocity as an operative principle of a life in common, involving not only exchange and fair-dealing but mutual respect and the free acceptance of mutual obligation.

These qualities generate norms, customs, habits, and traditions, which themselves give life to institutions as repositories of inherited wisdom at the disposal of each generation. Norman's claim that institutions "are bound together by affection, identity, and interest" suggests a more general claim that might be made about what makes an institution—or a social order—legitimate, or trusted, as we prefer to say today. The conditions of trust or legitimacy seem to be some combination of attachment, recognition, benefit, and reciprocity, varying with particular circumstances.

The attributes which make commercial society possible are found in abundance in ordinary daily life. For as long as we continue to be human, they will always be available to us at some closer or further distance, depending on whether we are attentive or complacent to cultivating them. The question for our moment is how well do conditions obtain *currently* for sustaining, recovering, or creating a commercial society? As Norman observes, we "seem to be becoming increasingly trapped in bleak and nihilistic narratives of grievance and anger . . . that ignore our history and devalue our society", and it is precisely as a way out of this trap that he proposes the idea of commercial society. The trap we have built for ourselves, however, is formidable. A settled tendency to ignore our history and to devalue our society favours Jacobinism, as Burke describes it, which despises the advantages we have and chooses to act as if we "had never been moulded into a civil society"; as if we had never been attached to or part of *anything*.

There are other trends pointing in the same worrying direction. Commercial society depends on interaction and empathy. Its prospects are not helped when there is a growing sense of isolation and disconnection, and when so much of public debate is framed in terms of enmity rather than sympathy. Norms of integrity and truth-telling are indispensable for commercial society. The breakdown of these norms has produced massive systems of compliance and regulation to oversee the conduct of individuals and institutions, and a significant degree of cynicism not only about whether experts and authorities can be trusted to provide truthful information, but also about whether anything beyond our own "personal truth" is possible or reliable. The "ceaseless exchange of mutual obligations and personal regard" which is at the centre of commercial society is threatened by an increasingly transactional approach to exchange, favouring exchange without obligation, and by a public culture relentlessly directed towards exposure and condemnation, rather than admiration and respect. Mutual obligation, except when invoked in an impoverished sense in matters of compliance or transaction, seems to be more and more elusive in a society where individual autonomy almost always prevails over the needs of others and the common good, and where certain formulations of diversity, tolerance, and identity cast profound doubt over whether human beings share anything in common at all.

Is Jacobinism the right word to use to describe this constellation of disenchantment and irrationalism? Norman's invocation of Burke on this point encourages us to think that it is. The use of this word may even be salutary, given the complacency of the Anglophone countries of the West about the durability of their procedural democracies and their tendency to condescension, even today, about political extremism as something which is only really a problem in other places, not at home. Writing about the fall of the communist regimes in central and eastern Europe at the end of the 1980s, S. N. Eisenstadt commented on "the tensions inherent in the cultural programs of modernity", not least "the tensions between the Jacobin and the liberal or pluralistic elements of this program". He reminds us that "Jacobin orientations, with their belief in the transformation of society through totalistic political action, are very modern", even if their roots go back to the Middle Ages. "The Jacobin element" can be found in many different forms of politics, including nationalism, populism, and fundamentalism, as well as communism and other forms of politics on the left.[2]

Most importantly for our purposes, Eisenstadt emphasises that the Jacobin element can be found in different guises—not only political—"in all modern societies, including those that are dem-ocratic-constitutional". It is true that while in totalitarian regimes the Jacobin element is given wider range, in democratic societies it is usually—or hitherto has usually been—"hemmed in", con-fined to being "only a single component in the overall pluralis-tic constitutional arrangements".[3] However, the emptying "of the centre ground" of politics in Western countries, which Norman acknowledges as one of the problems in a broader situation of breakdown and disintegration, means that the extremes grow in strength and set the agenda, reinforcing their appeal in the pro-cess, in a context where pluralistic constitutional arrangements and institutions seem to be losing authority, confidence, and com-petence.

If Jacobinism is a helpful concept for understanding the forces and passions diminishing the prospects of commercial society at this moment, there are clearly some important differences from its historical precursors. Perhaps the most significant is that con-temporary Jacobinism is not the grand narrative Jacobinism of the French or Bolshevik revolutions. The "transformation of society through totalistic political action", which Eisenstadt highlights as a central feature of Jacobinism in modern societies, is not its ob-ject today. Norman alludes to this feature of Jacobinism in the twentieth century when he describes how the freedom and equal-ity of a normal society can be "subsumed by the hierarchies and structures of an overwhelming collective goal". Jacobinism in the twenty-first century does not have one collective purpose. It aims neither at totality nor meaning. It is instead a series of ideological goals without coherence and often pointing in different directions, which enforce conformity without creating either a collective or any sense of purpose. The self-enforcement of the requirements necessary to meet these goals, spontaneously from within society as it were, with the state often only called on to provide secondary reinforcement once they have been well-established, is another notable feature of contemporary Jacobinism. Original Jacobinism used exposure and exclusion of 'the enemy' to create a spurious unity. The new Jacobinism uses exposure and exclusion to secure conformity and to deepen isolation at the same time, providing not even a tenuous sense of belonging or safety.

Suspicion was a large part of classical Jacobinism. It is part of the Jacobinism of the grey-zone as well. Robespierre made himself indispensable for a time by deepening suspicion of everyone, and establishing himself as the one who alone could penetrate to the truth. "Reality was not the truth but in fact masked the truth; it was opacity. What could be seen was not what really existed: reality was a lie". Facts were deceiving, and words no less so. Robespierre's "demystifying discourse", however, was itself "the work of a great illusionist". "Armed with the truth, Robespierre dispelled the shadows of reality and ripped away the veil of language. Through him, confusion became order, obscurity became clarity".[4] Our situation knows no Robespierre, thankfully, but the suspicion and mistrust of anything received and established; the sense that institutions and systems have failed, not least by lying to us, and that the future offers only catastrophe in one form or another, makes it easier for extremism to appear, as Robespierre presented it, as a moral necessity. While Robespierre could still appeal to the truth, in a context where truth is thought to be unknowable and appeals to fact and reason are viewed as a deception, the only reliable guide to what is true or the right thing to do becomes the intensity of our feelings. This leaves people susceptible to passivity on the one hand and paranoia on the other, as a sense of powerlessness and lack of agency alternates with a greater willingness to entertain conspiracy theories, or at the very least, to blame remote and powerful others and their system for all that is wrong.

All of which is a very long way away from "the ceaseless exchange of mutual obligations and personal regard" that gives commercial society its life and power. The contrast between commercial society and Jacobinism is stark, because the one is based on the humanness of the human condition, and the other on a derangement of it. Deranged times always fascinate, not only because of the drama and upheaval and destruction they wreak, but because of the possibilities they unleash—most enthralling of all being the possibility of finally transcending our condition on our own terms and by our own means.

The allure of this promise continues to be very powerful, even if it no longer takes grand narrative forms, but it can be resisted, as Burke and others resisted Jacobinism at the time of the French Revolution. Commercial society is not simply an alternative to Jacobinism but a model of how to resist it. Instead of contempt for people and their attachments, for the social order and the achievements of the past, commercial society begins with respect. Among other things, respect is a form of self-restraint, which might properly be likened to modesty in its regard for others and oneself.

Modesty does not sell so well today, but Jesse Norman is not afraid to pitch it as the foundation of successful leadership and politics, even in the midst of most immodest times. Like reasonableness, moderation, responsibility, and restraint, modesty is one of those qualities we rely on more than we wish to admit for making any sort of life in common humanly possible. When it is lacking, we lament it—but often find ourselves too engrossed in the drama and mayhem caused by the absence of what we might call the civil virtues to turn our minds seriously to their recovery.

In its own small way, perhaps this shows how contagious derangement can be, how imbued we too have become with the irresponsibility of the times. In opposition to this, commercial society puts the civil virtues at the centre of things, where they unobtrusively build up peace and flourishing. Norman's proposal for commercial society is put to us forthrightly, with great energy and clarity, as a means for resisting the Jacobin element that haunts us—if we have the sense and the will to grasp it. If, however, this should prove beyond us, the idea of commercial society still stands as a path for recovering a humane society, when, as in Luke's Gospel, the demons have gone from us and we find ourselves once again clothed and in our right minds.[5]

CONTRIBUTORS

Cris Abbu is the manager of policy and projects at the PM Glynn Institute, Australian Catholic University's public policy think-tank.

Tania Aspland is a professor and dean of education policy and strategy at Australian Catholic University.

Michael Casey is the director of the PM Glynn Institute.

David Corbett has researched and written for numerous think-tanks including the Legatum Institute in London, the Jubilee Centre in Cambridge, and the PM Glynn Institute in Sydney.

Michael Easson AM enjoys a lifelong association with the Australian labour movement, and is currently chair and co-founder of various businesses, including EG Funds Management and Willow Technology Corporation.

Damien Freeman is editor of the Kapunda Press at the PM Glynn Institute.

Parnell Palme McGuinness is managing director of Thought Broker and Agenda C, and a columnist for the *Australian Financial Review*.

Gregory Melleuish is a professor of history and political science at the University of Wollongong.

Adrian Pabst is a professor of politics at the University of Kent and the Sir Peter Lawler visiting fellow at the PM Glynn Institute.

Leanne Smith is the director of the Whitlam Institute within Western Sydney University.

Marc Stears is a professor of politics and director of the Sydney Policy Lab at the University of Sydney.

Tom Switzer is executive director of the Centre for Independent Studies in Sydney, a presenter on ABC's Radio National, and a columnist with the *Sydney Morning Herald*.

Amanda Walsh is the policy and government relations manager at Early Childhood Australia.

NOTES

FOREWORD

1   J. M. Keynes, "Economic Possibilities for our Grandchildren" (1930) in *Essays in Persuasion* (Norton, 1963), pp. 358-73.

2   B. Dolman, L. Lu and J. Rahman, "Understanding productivity trends", *Australian Treasury*, 2006 <https://treasury.gov.au/publication/economic-roundup-summer-2006/understanding-productivity-trends/>; G. Otto, "Productivity growth and economic policy in Australia", *Economic, Commerce and Industrial Relations Group Research Paper 19* (1996-97): <https://www.aph.gov.au/About_Parliament/Parliamentary_Departments/Parliamentary_Library/pubs/rp/RP9697/97rp19>.

3   Australian Bureau of Statistics, "Australian Labour Market Statistics": <http://www.abs.gov.au/ausstats/abs@.nsf/featurearticlesbytitle/67AB5016DD143FA-6CA2578680014A9D9?OpenDocument>.

A POLITICS OF EVERYDAY REALITY

1   See B. Honig, *Public Things: Democracy in Disrepair* (Fordham University Press, 2017).

BURKE VS SMITH ON NATURAL LAW, SOCIAL ORDER, AND SYMPATHY

1   J. Norman (ed.), The Achievement of Michael Oakeshott (Gerald Duckworth & Co, 1993); J. Norman and J. Ganesh, *Compassionate Conservatism: What it is—Why We Need it* (Policy Exchange, 2006); J. Norman, *Compassionate Economics: the social foundations of economic prosperity—a personal view* (Policy Exchange, 2008); J. Norman, *The Big Society: The Anatomy of the New Politics* University of Buckingham Press, 2010); J. Norman, "Conservative Free Markets, and the Case for Real Capitalism", December 2011, full text available at <https://jessenorman.typepad.com/Case_for_Real_Capitalism_28122011.pdf>; J. Norman, *Edmund Burke: The Visionary Who Invented Modern Politics* (Harpercollins, 2014); J. Norman, *Adam Smith: What He Thought, and Why it Matters* (Allan Lane, 2018).

2   E. Burke, *Reflections on the Revolution in France* in I. Hampsher-Monk (ed.), *Burke: Revolutionary Writings* (Cambridge University Press, 2014), p. 101.

3   Burke, *Reflections on the Revolution in France*, p. 63.

4   E. Burke, "The first Letter on a Regicide Peace" (1796) in *Burke: Revolutionary Writings*, pp. 316–17.

5   E. Burke, *Selected Writings and Speeches*, ed. P. J. Stanlis (Transaction Publishers, 2009), pp. 476, 478 and 479. In the words of Burke, "I must do justice to the East. I assert that their morality is equal to ours, in whatever regards the duties of governors, fathers, and superiors; and I challenge the world to show in any modern European book more true morality and wisdom than is to be found in the writings of Asiatic men in high trust, and who have been counsellors to princes. If this be the true morality of Asia, as I affirm and can prove that it is, the plea founded on Mr. Hasting's geographical morality is annihilated": *ibid.*, p. 480.

6   M. Freeman, *Edmund Burke and the Critique of Political Radicalism* (University of Chicago Press, 1980).

7   R. J. Vincent, "Edmund Burke and the theory of international relations", *Review of*

International Studies, Vol. 10(2), 1984, pp. 205–18, p. 207.

8 Burke, *Reflections on the Revolution in France*, p. 94.

9 E. Burke, "Religion" in I. Harris (ed.), *Burke: Pre-Revolutionary Writings* (Cambridge University Press, 1993), p. 82.

10 P. J. Stanlis, *Edmund Burke and the Natural Law* (University of Michigan Press, 1958).

11 Quoted in H. Barth, *The Idea of Order: Contributions to a Philosophy of Politics*, trans. E. W. Hankamer and W. M. Newell (Springer, 1960), p. 34.

12 E. Burke, *A Philosophical Enquiry into the Origin of our Ideas of the Sublime and Beautiful*, 2nd edn (1759), Part One, Sections VI–XIX, in *Burke: Pre-Revolutionary Writings*, p. 68.

13 Norman, *Edmund Burke: The Visionary Who Invented Modern Politics*, pp. 280 and 284.

14 A. Smith, *Theory of Moral Sentiments* (Prometheus, 2000), II, ii, 125.

15 A. Smith, *An Inquiry into the Nature and Causes of the Wealth of Nations* (Random Century, 1910), I, x, 2, p. 117.

16 L. Bruni and S. Zamagni, *Civil Economy: Efficiency, Equity, Public Happiness* (Peter Lang, 2007), p. 106 (original italics).

17 K. Haakonssen, *Natural Law and Moral Philosophy: From Grotius to the Scottish Enlightenment* (Cambridge University Press, 1996), pp. 180–81, 248–60.

18 Smith, *Theory of Moral Sentiments*, II, ii, 3, p. 124.

19 A. Sen, "Open and Closed Impartiality", *The Journal of Philosophy*, Vol. 99, 2002, pp. 445–69; A. Sen, "What Do We Want from A Theory of Justice?", *The Journal of Philosophy*, Vol. 103, 2006, pp. 215–38; A. Sen, "Adam Smith's Market Never Stood Alone", *Financial Times*, 11 March 2009; A. Sen, *The Idea of Justice* (Allen Lane, 2010), pp. 31–51, 124–52, 174–07, 388–416; K. Haakonssen and D. Winch, "The Legacy of Adam Smith", in K. Haakonssen (ed.), *The Cambridge Companion to Adam Smith* (Cambridge University Press, 2006), pp. 366–94; D. D. Raphael, *The Impartial Spectator: Adam Smith's moral philosophy* (Oxford University Press, 1973); E. Rothschild, *Economic Sentiments. Adam Smith, Condorcet, and the Enlightenment* (Harvard University Press, 2001); A. S. Skinner, *A System of Social Science: Papers Relating to Adam Smith* (Oxford University Press, 1996), esp. pp. 123–44; D. Winch and P. O'Brien (eds), *The Political Economy of British Historical Experience, 1688–1914* (Oxford University Press, 2002); G. Arrighi, *Adam Smith in Beijing. Lineages of the Twenty-First Century* (Verso, 2007), pp. 1–68.

20 J. Milbank and A. Pabst, *The Politics of Virtue: Post-liberalism and the Human Future* (Rowman & Littlefield International, 2016).

21 A. Pabst, *The Demons of Liberal Democracy* (Polity, 2019).

22 M. Midgley, *The Ethical Primate: Humans, Freedom and Morality* (Routledge, 1994), p. 134.

BURKE AND AUSTRALIAN BRITISHNESS

1 G. Melleuish, "Has Menzies' Liberal Party run its course?", *Meanjin*, Vol. 78(1), Autumn 2019, pp. 106-112.

2 D. Kemp, *A Free Country: Australians Search for Utopia: 1861—1901* (Melbourne University Press, 2019), pp. 35-36.

3 J. Allan, *Democracy in Decline: Steps in the Wrong Direction*, Kindle edition (McGill-Queens University Press, 2014), Location 775—895.

4 S. Chavura and G. Melleuish, "Conservative instinct in Australian political thought:

The Federation debates, 1890–1898", *Australian Journal of Political Science,* Vol. 50(3), 2015, p. 525.

5 S. Piggin and R. D. Linder, *The Fountain of Public Prosperity: Evangelical Christians in Australian History 1740—1914* (Monash University Press, 2018). See also D. Kemp, *The Land of Dreams: How Australians won their Freedom 1788—1860* (Melbourne University Press, 2018).

6 J. Hirst, *The Strange Birth of Colonial Democracy* (Allen & Unwin, 1988), p. 17.

7 C. H. Spence, *An Autobiography*, p. 56. Available at: <http://www.gutenberg.org/files/4220/4220-h/4220-h.htm>.

8 D. Malouf, "Made in England: Australia's British Inheritance", *Quarterly Essay*, No 12, 2003, pp. 1-66.

9 E. Burke, "Speech on moving his Resolutions on Conciliation with America" in *Works*, Vol. 3 (Rivington, 1815), pp. 49-50.

10 *John West's 'Union Among the Colonies'*, ed. G. Melleuish (Australian Scholarly Publishing, 2001), p. 16.

11 W. G. McMinn, *A Constitutional History of Australia* (Oxford University Press, 1979), pp. 59-61.

12 W. K. Hancock, *Australia* (Ernest Benn, 1930), p. 53.

13 J. B. Chifley, "To the People of Britain—the Proud Admiration of the Australian People" in A. W. Stargardt (ed), *Things Worth Fighting For: Speeches by Joseph Benedict Chifley* (Melbourne University Press, 1952), pp. 128-30.

14 See Chavura and Melleuish, "Conservative instinct in Australian political thought".

15 J. Belich, *Replenishing the Earth: The Settler Revolution and the Rise of the Anglo-World, 1783—1939* (Oxford University Press, 2009), pp. 456-78.

16 H. Parkes, *Mr Gladstone and English Liberalism from an Australian point of view* (Lee and Ross, 1878).

17 G. Melleuish, "Beneficent Providence and the Quest for Harmony: The Cultural Setting for Colonial Science in Sydney 1850–1890", *Journal and Proceedings, Royal Society of New South Wales*, Vol. 118, 1985, pp. 167-80.

18 J. H. Newman, *Apologia Pro Vita Sua* (Collins, 1977), p. 113.

19 Kemp, *The Land of Dreams*, pp. 120-26.

20 G. Melleuish, "Colonial Government" in B. Galligan and W. Roberts (eds), *The Oxford Companion to Australian Politics* (Oxford University Press, 2007), pp. 112-14.

21 H. Mansfield, *Statesmanship and Party Government: A Study of Burke and Bolingbroke* (University of Chicago Press, 1965).

22 *Official Report of the National Australasian Convention debates* (George Stephen Chapman, Acting Government Printers, 1891), p. 915.

23 Chavura and Melleuish, "Conservative instinct in Australian political thought".

24 Z. Gorman and G. Melleuish, "The nexus clause: a peculiarly Australian obstacle", *Cogent Arts and Humanities*, vol. 5(1), 2018.

25 G. Melleuish, *Despotic State or Free Individual: Two Traditions of Democracy in Australia* (Australian Scholarly Publishing, 2014), p. 43.

26 J. Brett, "Class, Religion and the Foundation of the Australian Party System: A Revisionist Interpretation", *Australian Journal of Political Science*, Vol. 57(1), 2002, pp. 39-56.

27 A. A. Calwell, *Labor's Role in Modern Society* (Landsdowne Press, 1965), p. 39.

28 Melleuish, *Despotic State or Free Individual*, pp. 152-66.

29 G. Melleuish, "Burke Down Under", *Dorchester Review*, Vol. 5(1), 2015, pp. 44-48.

30 G. Melleuish, "Constitution and Culture: the unusual case of Australia" in *Telos*, 189, WInter 2019.

31 M. Oakeshott, *Rationalism in politics and other essays* (Liberty Fund, 1991), pp. 5-42.

32 Allan, *Democracy in Decline.*

33 I. Kramnick, *Bolingbroke and His Circle: The politics of Nostalgia in the Age of Walpole* (Cornell University Press, 1992).

34 H. St J. Bolingbroke, *The Idea of a Patriot King*, available at: <https://socialsciences.mcmaster.ca/econ/ugcm/3ll3/bolingbroke/king.html>.

BURKE AND AUSTRALIAN LABOR

1 In common with Australian usage, it is the 'Labor Party' and the 'labour movement'.

2 Specifically, J. W. Howard, *Lazarus Rising: A Personal and Political Autobiography* (Harper Collins Publishers, 2010), pp. 200 and 654.

3 J. Norman, *Edmund Burke: Philosopher, Politician, Prophet* (William Collins, 2013); for a critique: M. Easson, "Burke's Great Melody Against It" [review of Norman's book], *The Oxonian Review*, Vol. 24(4), 3 March 2014.

4 Interestingly, a study of the emergence of Burke's reputation, E. Jones, *Edmund Burke & the Invention of Modern Conservatism, 1830-1914: An Intellectual History* (Oxford University Press, 2017), argues that "a distilled political theory was gradually extracted from his corpus and de-contextualized accordingly." (p. 229). And thus the interpretation of Burke as a conservative was born. Yet "this apparently neat intellectual and political legacy is in fact modern, the product of a long historical process" (p. 2).

5 Though even within fifty years of Burke's death, "conservativism, liberalism, and radicalism . . . took on many new meanings", J. G. A. Pocock, Introduction to Edmund Burke, *Reflections on the Revolution in France* (1790), (Hackett Publishing Company, 1987), p. xl.

6 Cf. E. Burke, *An Appeal from the New to the Old Whigs in Consequence of Some Late Discussions in Parliament Relative to the Reflections on the French Revolution* (J. Dodsley, 1791).

7 J. Morley, *On Compromise* (Chapman and Hall, 1874), p. 168.

8 J. Morley, *Edmund Burke: An Historical Study* (Macmillan & Co., 1867), p. 9.

9 Hence, some writers like Pocock, and D. Bromwich, *The Intellectual Life of Edmund Burke: From the Sublime and Beautiful to American Independence* (Belnap Press, 2014) argue about the radical liberal, pro-liberty aspects of Burke's thought. But here is not the place to re-litigate his legacy. It is enough to note the argument.

10 For example, Burke's argument that: "Your representative owes you, not his industry only, but his judgment: and he betrays instead of serving you if he sacrifices it to your opinion" is cited by Barry Jones, Member for Lalor, *Hansard*, House of Representatives, 22 March 1979; Nick Champion, Member for Wakefield, *Hansard*, House of Representatives, 10 September 2012; Michael Danby, Member for Melbourne Ports, *Hansard*, House of Representatives, 2 April 2019.

11 <www.thescribefilm.com>.

12 Email: Ross Garnaut to Michael Easson, 23 December 2018. *Reflections* being Burke's polemic *Reflections on the Revolution in France* (1790).

13 B. Jones, "Relevance of the French Revolution in 2016" in his *Knowledge. Courage. Leadership* (Wilkinson Publishing, 2016), p. 241. The 'organic' refers to Burke's idea, stated in *Reflections on the Revolution in France* (1790) that society is a "partnership not only between those who are living, but between those who

are living, those who are dead, and those who are to be born." What was prophetic was Burke's prediction in the first edition of *Reflections* that the monarch would be executed and a bloody terror would ensue.

14 The classic study of the period, accounting for party division and splits, is R. Murray, *The Split* (F.W. Cheshire, 1970). See also, R. Murray, *Labor and Santamaria* (Australian Scholarly, 2016); M. Easson, "Labor and Santamaria" [review of the Murray book], *Recorder: Official Organ of the Melbourne Branch of the Australian Society for the Study of Labour History*, No. 288, March 2017, p. 7.

15 The history of various Labor sub-factions is poorly explored in the Australian academic literature.

16 G. Healey, "ALP", *The Story of the Labor Party* (Jacaranda Press, 1955), p. 226.

17 In 2004 the Labor Council of NSW was renamed Unions NSW, the peak body of the unions in NSW.

18 On the NSW ALP Right tradition, see: M. Easson, "Right Approach for a Tired Party", *The Australian*, 8 December 2012.

19 B. Nairn, *Civilising Capitalism. The Labor Movement in New South Wales 1870-1900* (Australian National University Press, 1973).

20 M. Easson, "What It Means to be Labor" in M. Easson (ed.), *The Foundations of Labor* (Pluto Press and the Lloyd Ross Forum, 1990), pp. 72-73.

21 In private conversation with the author, the Labor intellectual and lawyer John McCarthy QC called this 'bonapartist' leadership. The phrase is suggestive, though if small-b bonapartist leadership sounds too authoritarian, that falsely paints the scene. (Of course there is irony with the phrase in an essay referencing Edmund Burke, who thought that a dictator would emerge out of revolutionary France.)

22 The impressively produced (though never continued) *Labor Year Book 1973*, ed. C. Wagner, (Mass Communications Australia on behalf of the NSW ALP & the Labor Council of NSW, 1973), which, at the time I closely thumbed through, contained a wealth of information on sitting ALP members in the Federal and NSW parliaments. The preponderance of Catholics in Sydney was particularly obvious.

23 The internal party coups against Premier Morris Iemma (2008) and Kevin Rudd (2010) partly shattered this tradition. It was noticeable that, in consequence, party membership dropped off, melting away in some places.

24 H. M. Drucker, *Doctrine and Ethos in the Labour Party* (George Allen & Unwin, 1979), p. 25.

25 In a British context, see: P. Akers and A. J. Reid (eds), *Alternatives to State-Socialism in Britain: Other Worlds of Labour in the Twentieth Century* (Palgrave Macmillan, 2016) and a review, M. Easson, *Labour History*, No. 114, May 2018, pp. 197-198.

26 Drucker, *passim*, but particularly pp. vii-viii; 1-43.

27 E. Burke, "Speech on Conciliation with America" (22 March 1775) in *The Works of The Right Honourable Edmund Burke in twelve volumes*, Vol. 2 (John C. Nimmo, 1887), pp. 168-169.

28 *Ibid.*, p. 169.

29 On Machiavelli, the contrast between the 'real', the mythologised and corrupted, see: M. Jackson and D. Grace, *Machiavelliana: The Living Machiavelli in Modern Mythologies* (Brill-Rodopi, 2018).

30 Without any chase to this rabbit, the emphasis on tradition, faith and family is part of the argument of Blue Labour in the UK. See: I. Geary and A. Pabst (eds), *Blue Labour: Forging a New Politics* (I.B. Tauris, 2015), particularly the chapter by

Luke Bretherton on "Faith and Family".

31 D. Marquand, "My Hero: Edmund Burke", *The Guardian*, 11 September 2010. This too is the argument—on Burke's consistent opposition to tyranny, his great melody against, in one of the best biographies of Burke, C. C. O'Brien, *The Great Melody: A Thematic Biography of Edmund Burke* (Sinclaire-Stevenson, 1992).

32 M. Easson, "The Liberalism of Richard Bourke", *Quadrant*, Vol. 62(11), November 2018, pp. 54-58. In retirement Bourke co-edited his uncle's letters. See: *Correspondence of The Right Honourable Edmund Burke*, C. William, Earl Fitzwilliam, and Sir Richard Bourke (eds) (Francis & John Rivington, 1844), in four volumes.

33 Bourke's *Church Act* (1836) disestablished the Church of England and provided funding support for the major Christian denominations; the small Jewish congregation also received limited state support. The first synagogue was formally established in 1837. Bourke's reforms were enacted despite stormy opposition from among various protestant religious leaders. See D. Kenny, *Progress of Catholicity in Australia* (F. Cunninghame & Co., 1886), pp. 106-114.

34 Richard Bourke quipped that as Governor at times he felt "pretty much in the situation that Earl Grey would find himself in if all members of his Cabinet were Ultra Tories and he could neither turn them out nor leave them", with the conservatives in the New South Wales Legislative Council seeking to block his reforms. The quote is cited in H. King, "Bourke, Sir Richard (1777-1855)", *Australian Dictionary of Biography* (Melbourne University Press, 1966), Vol. 1, p. 130.

35 G. Freudenberg, *Cause for Power: The Official History of the New South Wales Branch of the Australian Labor Party* (Pluto Press, 1991), p. 3.

36 *Ibid.*

37 B. Nairn, p. 165.

38 *Ibid.*

39 C. M. H. Clark, *A History of Australia. Volume V: The People Make Laws 1888-1915* (Melbourne University Press, 1981), p. 187.

40 V. G. Childe, *How Labour Governs: a Study in Workers' Representation in Australia* (The Labour Publishing Company, 1923), p. 74. Note "Labour" rather than "Labor" because the book was published in England.

41 *Ibid.*, p. 85.

42 See: T. H. Irving, "On the Work of Labour Governments: Vere Gordon Child's Plans for Volume Two of *How Labour Governs*" in P. Gathercole, T. H. Irving and G. Melleuish (eds), *Childe and Australia. Archeology, Politics and Ideas* (University of Queensland Press, 1995), pp. 82-94.

43 E. Burke, *Reflections on the Revolution in France* (1790), J. G. A. Pocock (ed.), (Hackett, 1987), p. 31. Emphasis in the original.

44 Cf. M. Lake, *Progressive New World: How Colonialism and Transpacific Exchange Shaped American Reform* (Harvard University Press, 2019), pp. 106-135; 193-223.

45 E. O'Connor, "Hail Russia! Labour and the Bolshevik Revolution", *Saothar*, No. 42, 2017, pp. 107-114. Admittedly, the call for violent uprising might have appealed more in Ireland, than say Canada, caught up as Ireland was in rebellion and then Civil War.

46 When Curtin took ill before the 1921 ALP national conference in Brisbane, Bob Ross was his nominee to replace him. See: Llyod Ross, *John Curtin: A Biography* (MacMillan, 1977), p. 75.

47 R. S. Ross, *Revolution in Russia and Australia* (Ross's Book Service, 1920).

48 This is a neglected area of analysis and deserves further research, which the author

plans to undertake.

49 G. Evans, "Reshaping the Socialist Objective", in B. O'Meagher (ed.), *The Socialist Objective: Labor & Socialism* (Hale & Iremonger, 1983), p. 64.

50 Note that the UK Labour's Clause 4 of its Constitution, adopted in 1918 (repealed in 1995), resolved: "To secure for the workers by hand or by brain the full fruits of their industry and the most equitable distribution thereof that may be possible upon the basis of the common ownership of the means of production, distribution and exchange, and the best obtainable system of popular administration and control of each industry or service."

51 M. Atkinson, "Whither Goes Labour", *Steads Review* (Australian Edition), Vol. 58(12), 9 December 1922, p. 16.

52 *ibid.*

53 R. S. Ross, "A Reply" [to an article in the same issue of the journal on "Panaceas. V. Revolution: Australian Way"], *Steads Review* (Australian Edition), Vol. 56(5), 3 September 1921, p. 260.

54 *Ibid.*

55 Unfortunately a discussion in a recent biography on the origins of and the thinking behind the Blackburn Declaration is so truncated as to be unilluminating: C. Rasmussen, *The Blackburns. Private Lives, Public Ambitions* (Melbourne University Press, 2019), pp. 167-169. Blackburn was expelled from the ALP in 1935, then re-admitted and expelled again in 1941, three years before he died, for drifting too close to the communists. Ironic then, that the Blackburn Declaration was so popular with certain Labor moderates.

56 F. McManus, *The Tumult and the Shouting* (Rigby, 1977), pp. 143-144. *Freedom* was then the newspaper of the Catholic Social Studies Movement. McManus was the Assistant Secretary of the ALP, Victorian Branch, to 1954, and subsequently a Democratic Labor Party Senator for Victoria.

57 B. Chifley, "The Labour Movement Lives by the Work of All In It", An Address to the Federal Executive of the Australian Labor Party, 5 October 1949, in A. W. Stargardt (ed.), *Things Worth Fighting For. Speeches by Joseph Benedict Chifley* (Melbourne University Press, 1952), p. 71.

58 R. Mathews, *Of Labour and Liberty: Distribution in Victoria 1891-1966* (Monash University Publishing, 2017), and for a review: M. Easson, *Journal of the Australian Catholic Historical Society*, Vol. 38, 2017, pp. 158-162.

59 For example, L. Ross, "Labour, Catholicism, and Democratic Socialism", *Twentieth Century*, Vol. 2(2), December 1947, pp. 74-89. Mathews and Ross, both atheists, saw Catholic social thinking as complementary to social democracy.

60 The Hawke government restored the universal health insurance system that was originally the work of the Minister for Social Security Bill Hayden in the Labor government of Prime Minister Gough Whitlam. Originally called Medibank, the system came into being after the passing of legislation by a joint sitting of Parliament on 7 August 1974. After certain emasculating changes under the Fraser, Liberal Country Party Coalition government, the Hawke government re-instated the original model, under the new name Medicare. See: R. B. Scotton and C. R. Macdonald, *The Making of Medibank* (School of Health Services Management, University of New South Wales, 1993).

61 Specifically, the concept that good policy is developed in sympathy with the living, the dead, and those to be born. See: M. Easson, *Keating's and Kelty's Super Legacy: The Birth and Relentless Threats to the Australian System of Superannuation* (Con-

nor Court Publishing, 2017), p. 213 (which cites Burke), and fn. 13 above.

62 This is from memory. The Amalgamated Metal Workers' Union, "the metal workers", was prominent in this debate. Some contemporary press articles include: "Keating's Passionate Plea for More Banks", *Sydney Morning Herald*, 11 June 1984, p. 5; "Foreign banks 'a benefit'", *The Canberra Times*, 12 June 1984, p. 9.

63 P.J. Keating, "Traditions of Labor in Power; Whitlam and Hawke in the Continuum" in S. Loosley (ed.), *Traditions for Reform in New South Wales: Labor History Essays* (Pluto Press, 1987, 1987), p.186.

Markets, Morals and Australian Labor Governments

1   D. Hodson and D. Mabbett, "UK economic policy and the global financial crisis: paradigm lost?", *Journal of Common Market Studies*, Vol. 47(5), 2009, pp. 1042, 1052.

2   K. Murphy, "Ten years on, voters say Labor's $52bn stimulus saved Australia from recession", *The Guardian Australia*, 4 August 2017.

3   Reserve Bank of Australia, "The Global Financial Crisis" (2019): <https://www.rba.gov.au/education/resources/explainers/the-global-financial-crisis.html>.

4   D. Harvey, *A Brief History of Neoliberalism* (Oxford University Press, 2005), p. 20.

5   F. Stilwell, *The Accord and beyond: the political economy of the Labor government* (Pluto Press, 1986), p. 11.

6   A. Walsh, *Globalisation, the state and regional Australia* (Sydney University Press, 2018), p. 55.

7   Australian Labor Party, *ALP National Platform* (ALP, 2018), p. 13.

8   D. Cahill, *The end of laissez-faire? On the durability of embedded liberalism* (Edward Elgar, 2014).

The limits of natural utility

1   H. Taylor-Mill, "The Enfranchisement of Women", *The Westminster Review*, 1851.

2   See for example, Mandeville or Rousseau, both of whom argued that commercial society was instead characterized by a psychopathy—that citizens can be good or wealthy, not both.

3   "The Three Evils", speech delivered at the National Conference on New Politics, 31 August 1967, Chicago, Il.

4   <https://www.gov.uk/government/news/social-mobility-in-great-britain-fifth-state-of-the-nation-report>.

5   "At least 32,000 homeless people in Britain says shelter", *The Guardian*, 22 November 2018.

6   <https://www.britannica.com/topic/social-democracy>.

7   P. Beilharz, "Australian Laborism, Social Democracy, and Social Justice", *Social Justice*, Vol. 16(3), 1989, pp. 15–29.

8   J. Dewey, "The Place of the Self and the Social in the Moral Life", *Ethics*, 1932.

Constraints to market exchange

1   R. Hanley, "Adam Smith and human flourishing", *Economic Freedom and Human Flourishing: Essay Series* (American Enterprise Institute, 2019) <http://www.aei.org/spotlight/human-flourishing-adam-smith/>; P. Sagar, "The real Adam Smith", AEON, 2018, <https://aeon.co/essays/we-should-look-closely-at-what-adam-

smith-actually-believed>; R. Sirico, "Defending the free market: The moral case for a free economy", *Business Economics*, Vol. 48(2), 2013, p. 144.

2   Department of Human Services, "Understanding NDIS", 2018 <https://www.ndis. gov.au/understanding>; Productivity Commission, "Disability Care and Support", Report no. 54, 2011.

IN PRAISE OF PARTNERSHIP

1   L. von Mises, *Economic Policy: Thoughts for Today and Tomorrow Capitalism* (Ludwig von Mises Institute, 2006).

2   They authored various Marxist works, e.g.: M. Weber, *Die protestantische Ethik und der Geist des Kapitalismus* (published in English as *The Protestant Ethic and the Spirit of Capitalism*), 1st edn (1904); W. Sombart, *The Quintessence of Capitalism: a study of the history and psychology of the modern business man* (E. P. Dutton, 1915)

3   M. Mahendra, "Impact of Karl Marx on scholarly World: A Scientometric Study" in P. K. Jain (ed), *Emerging Trends and Issues in Scientometrics Informetrics and Webometrics* (Ane Books, 2015), pp. 533-536.

4   K. Marx, *Das Kapital* (Progress Publishers,1954-59), Vol. 1, Ch. XXIV.

5   J. D. Heydon, *Heydon on Contract: the general part* (LexisNexis, 2019).

6   "'Societãs' (classical Latin), in English "society"—definition: being associated for a common purpose, a partnership . . .": *The Oxford English Dictionary.*

7   Rousseau uncritically praised contract. Burke pointed to partnership between young and old. As there can be no voluntary agreement between the dead and the living, Burke's 'contract' between the living and the dead is not strictly a contract in the sense of a voluntary agreement. It is a form of partnership.

8   There is good reason to say that 'mutual society' may even be the main reason for marriage (though in many ways all its purposes are indivisible). The case for its primacy can be argued from the Scriptures. The very reason for creating the two sexes was "it is not good for man to be alone" (Genesis 2:18) therefore companionship was at the core of the world's design (despite the legal definition of marriage now extending to other sexes too, mutual society might still be its main reason, in fact this new formulation might be saying that 'mutual society and affection' is the only reason for marriage though mutual society must be the first reason amongst equals). The reason the 'mutual society' purpose for marriage is often missed may be because the definition of 'marriage' in the church, and its canon law, was originally Roman civil law. The civil law which was founded on the biological, not theological, reasons for marriage (namely, the practical consequences of sexual intercourse is children and therefore marriage is a protective structure for both the woman and child's benefit against capricious men). The married family in fact might be the prototype for all mutual societies. It is through the family individuals are reared into a form of mutual society. A Christian family, the subject of the Prayer Book, may be to take this further—to prepare for mutual society both human and, ultimately, heavenly. 'Mutual society' is therefore a very important component of marriage, and perhaps the prime reason for it.

9   *Heydon v NRMA Ltd & Ors; Bateman & Ors v NRMA Ltd & Ors; Morgan & Ors v NRMA Ltd & Ors* [2000] NSWCA 374; 51 NSWLR 1 at [7].

10 See: N. Skelton, *Constructive Conservatism* (The Spectator, 1923).

11 Distinguished works to help further this process are: P. Blonde, *Red Tory: How the*

Left and Right Have Broken Britain and How We Can Fix It (Faber & Faber, 2010); and I. Geary and A. Pabst (eds), *Blue Labour: Forging a New Politics* (I.B. Tauris, 2015).

MORAL RENEWAL AMIDST POLITICAL CHAOS

1   O. Harries, "What conservatism means," *Policy: the journal of the Centre for Independent Studies*, Winter, 2003.

QUESTIONS FOR THE ACADEMY IN AUSTRALIA

1   "Australia doesn't protect free speech", *The Conversation*, 7 June 2019: <http://theconversation.com/australia-doesnt-protect-free-speech-but-it-could-118448>.

2   Michael Kirby speaking on The Drum, 7 June 2019: <https://www.abc.net.au/news/2019-06-06/the-drum-thursday-june-6/11188040>.

3   S. Cohen, *Folk Devils and Moral Panics: The Creation of the Mods and Rockers* (Basil Blackwell, 1987).

4   S. Hall, C. Critcher, T. Jefferson and J.Clarke, *Policing the Crisis: Mugging, the State, and Law and Order* (Macmillan Press, 1978), p. 52.

5   F. Allon and J. Martin, "Panic in the streets: Homes, homelessness and public spaces", *Media International Australia*, Vol. 85(1), 1997, p. 24.

6   B. Massumi (ed.), *The Politics of Everyday Fear* (University of Minnesota Press, 1993), pp 3-37.

7   Allon and Martin, p. 24.

8   T. Aspland and F. Patel, "Enabling Leadership in Teaching and Learning: Balancing Creativity and Compliance Agendas in Australian Higher Education", *International Leadership Journal*, Vol. 6, 2014, pp 23-44.

9   M. Staub, "The Commonwealth of universities", paper presented at Worldwide Universities Network Conference, 13 March 2009.

10   V. I. Meek, "Diversity and marketisation of higher education: Incompatible concepts?", *Higher Education Policy*, Vol. 13(1), 2000, pp 23-39.

11   D. Seidman, "Four pillars of moral leadership", *Fortune* , 15 September 2017: <https://lrn.com/thought_leadership/four-pillars-of-moral-leadership-is-part-of-fortunes-2017-change-the-world-issue/>.

12   <http://www.acu.edu.au/about_acu/our_university/catholic_identity   April 20,2018>.

13   B. J. Caldwell and J. M. Spinks, *Leading the self-managing school: Education Policy Perspectives* (The Falmer Press, 1992), p. 50.

14   J. M. Burns, *Leadership* (Harper & Row, 1978).

15   J. D. Kenny, "Managing a modern university: is it time for a rethink?", *Higher Education Research & Development*, Vol. 28(6), 2009, pp 629-642, p. 633. See also Aspland and Patel (2014); S. Clegg and J. McAuley, "Conceptualising middle management in higher education: A multifaceted discourse", *Journal of Higher Education Policy and Management*, Vol. 27(1), 2005, pp 19-34; G. Patterson, "The applicability of institutional goals to the university organisation", *Journal of Higher Education Policy and Management*, Vol. 23(2), 2001, pp 159-169.

16   D. Twale and B. M. de Luca, *Faculty Incivility: The Rise of the Academic Bully Culture and What to Do About* (Wiley and Sons, 2011).

17   G. Weiner, "Auditing failure: Moral competence and school effectiveness", *British Educational Research Journal*, Vol. 26(6), 2002, pp 789-804.

18 Zapf & Einarsen, (2003) Individual antecedents of bullying: Victims and perpetrators. In: Einarsen, S., Hoel, H., Zapf, D. and Cooper C.L. Eds., Bullying and Emotional Abuse in the Workplace. International perspectives in research and practice. Taylor & Francis, London, 165-184

19 Aspland and Patel, *op. cit.*

20 B. Dzeich and L. Weiner, *The lecherous professor*, 2nd edn (University of Illinois Press, 1990).

21 Himes, K.R (2018) Modern Catholic Social Teaching. Boston: Georgetown Press.

22 Hall *et al*, *op. cit.*

23 Seidman, *op. cit.*

24 Sergiovanni, T.J. (1992). *Moral Leadership: Getting to the Heart of School Improvement*. San Francisco, CA: Jossey Bass.

25 Seidman, *op. cit.*

26 C. M. Branson, M. Marra, M. Franken, and D. Penney, "The Theoretical Foundations of Transrelational Leadership" in *Leadership in Higher Education from a Transrelational Perspective: Perspectives on Leadership in Higher Education* (Bloomsbury Academic, 2018), pp 35–59.

27 C. M. Branson, M. Franken and D. Penney, "Reconceptualising middle leadership in higher education: a transrelational approach" in J. McNiff (ed.), *Values and virtues in higher education research: Critical perspectives* (Routledge, 2016).

28 Staub, *op. cit.*

COMMERCIAL SOCIETY AND THE JACOBINS

1 See Furet's entry on "Jacobinism" in F. Furet and M. Ozouf, *A Critical Dictionary of the French Revolution*, trans. A. Goldhammer (Belknap Press: 1989).

2 S. N. Eisenstadt, "The Breakdown of Communist Regimes and the Vicissitudes of Modernity", *Daedalus*, Vol. 121(2), Spring 1992, p. 32.

3 *Ibid.*

4 P. Gueniffey, "Robespierre" in *A Critical Dictionary of the French Revolution*, pp. 303 and 305.

5 Luke 8:35: "Then people went out to see what happened, and they came to Jesus, and found the man from whom the demons had gone, sitting at the feet of Jesus, clothed and in his right mind; and they were afraid."

INDEX